Culture and Customs of Rwanda

Map of Rwanda. Cartography by Bookcomp, Inc.

Culture and Customs of Rwanda

JULIUS O. ADEKUNLE

Culture and Customs of Africa
Toyin Falola, Series Editor

GREENWOOD PRESS
Westport, Connecticut • London

Dedicated to the people of Rwanda.

Library of Congress Cataloging-in-Publication Data

Adekunle, Julius.
   Culture and customs of Rwanda / Julius O. Adekunle.
      p. cm. — (Culture and customs of Africa, ISSN 1530–8367)
   Includes bibliographical references and index.
   ISBN-13: 978–0–313–33177–0 (alk. paper)
   ISBN-10: 0–313–33177–4 (alk. paper)
  1. Rwanda—Civilization.   2. Rwanda—Social life and customs.   I. Title.
   DT450.23.A33   2007
   967.571—dc22   2007004341

British Library Cataloguing in Publication Data is available.

Library of Congress Catalog Card Number: 2007004341
ISBN-13: 978–0–313–33177–0
ISBN-10: 0–313–33177–4
ISSN: 1530–8367

First published in 2007

Greenwood Press, 88 Post Road West, Westport, CT 06881
An imprint of Greenwood Publishing Group, Inc.
www.greenwood.com

Printed in the United States of America

The paper used in this book complies with the
Permanent Paper Standard issued by the National
Information Standards Organization (Z39.48–1984).

10 9 8 7 6 5 4 3 2 1

The publisher has done its best to make sure the instructions and/or recipes in this book are correct. However, users should apply judgment and experience when preparing recipes, especially parents and teachers working with young people. The publisher accepts no responsibility for the outcome of any recipe included in this volume.

Contents

Series Foreword	vii
Preface	ix
Acknowledgments	xi
Abbreviations	xiii
Chronology	xv
1 Introduction	1
2 Religion and Worldview	27
3 Literature and Media	47
4 Art and Architecture/Housing	63
5 Cuisine and Traditional Dress	81
6 Gender Roles, Marriage, and Family	97
7 Social Customs and Lifestyle	115
8 Music and Dance	133
Appendix: Rwanda National Anthem and English Translation	147
Glossary	149
Bibliography	153
Index	159

Series Foreword

Africa is a vast continent, the second largest, after Asia. It is four times the size of the United States, excluding Alaska. It is the cradle of human civilization. A diverse continent, Africa has more than fifty countries with a population of over 700 million people who speak over 1,000 languages. Ecological and cultural differences vary from one region to another. As an old continent, Africa is one of the richest in culture and customs, and its contributions to world civilization are impressive indeed.

Africans regard culture as essential to their lives and future development. Culture embodies their philosophy, worldview, behavior patterns, arts, and institutions. The books in this series intend to capture the comprehensiveness of African culture and customs, dwelling on such important aspects as religion, worldview, literature, media, art, housing, architecture, cuisine, traditional dress, gender, marriage, family, lifestyles, social customs, music, and dance.

The uses and definitions of "culture" vary, reflecting its prestigious association with civilization and social status, its restriction to attitude and behavior, its globalization, and the debates surrounding issues of tradition, modernity, and postmodernity. The participating authors have chosen a comprehensive meaning of culture while not ignoring the alternative uses of the term.

Each volume in the series focuses on a single country, and the format is uniform. The first chapter presents a historical overview, in addition to information on geography, economy, and politics. Each volume then proceeds to examine the various aspects of culture and customs. The series highlights the mechanisms for the transmission of tradition and culture across generations:

the significance of orality, traditions, kinship rites, and family property distribution; the rise of print culture; and the impact of educational institutions. The series also explores the intersections between local, regional, national, and global bases for identity and social relations. While the volumes are organized nationally, they pay attention to ethnicity and language groups and the links between Africa and the wider world.

The books in the series capture the elements of continuity and change in culture and customs. Custom is represented not as static or as a museum artifact but as a dynamic phenomenon. Furthermore, the authors recognize the current challenges to traditional wisdom, which include gender relations, the negotiation of local identities in relation to the state, the significance of struggles for power at national and local levels and their impact on cultural traditions and community-based forms of authority, and the tensions between agrarian and industrial/manufacturing/oil-based economic modes of production.

Africa is a continent of great changes, instigated mainly by Africans but also through influences from other continents. The rise of youth culture, the penetration of the global media, and the challenges to generational stability are some of the components of modern changes explored in the series. The ways in which traditional (non-Western and nonimitative) African cultural forms continue to survive and thrive—that is, how they have taken advantage of the market system to enhance their influence and reproductions—also receive attention.

Through the books in this series, readers can see their own cultures in a different perspective, understand the habits of Africans, and educate themselves about the customs and cultures of other countries and people. The hope is that the readers will come to respect the cultures of others and see them not as inferior or superior to theirs but merely as different. Africa has always been important to Europe and the United States, essentially as a source of labor, raw materials, and markets. Blacks are in Europe and the Americas as part of the African diaspora, a migration that took place primarily because of the slave trade. Recent African migrants increasingly swell their number and visibility. It is important to understand the history of the diaspora and the newer migrants as well as the roots of the culture and customs of the places from where they come. It is equally important to understand others in order to be able to interact successfully in a world that keeps shrinking. The accessible nature of the books in this series will contribute to this understanding and enhance the quality of human interaction in a new millennium.

Toyin Falola
Frances Higginbothom Nalle Centennial Professor in History
The University of Texas at Austin

Preface

Rwanda is a country bestowed with beautiful physical features. Early European travelers attested to its beauty by describing it variously as "a land of almost ideal beauty," "the Switzerland of Africa," and "the Pearl of Africa." Rwanda also has been referred to as "the Land of a Thousand Hills" and "the Land of Gorillas." Its spectacular volcanoes, mountains, and natural resources are significant economic assets to the country. In spite of its long history as well as natural and physical beauty, however, not much has been written about Rwanda's culture and customs.

A series of sociopolitical problems facing Rwanda culminated in the ethnic conflict that occurred in 1994. That unfortunate incident placed the international limelight on Rwanda and thrust the country onto the global stage. Rwanda became a focus of attention for international political thinkers as well as world organizations. Although Rwanda possesses a long history, not much was heard about it on the world scene until 1994.

Still recognized as "the Land of a Thousand Hills" and "the Land of Gorillas," Rwanda has become known as "the Land of Violence" and "the Land of Genocide." The nation has experienced several sociopolitical vicissitudes, including differences and inequalities between the ethnic groups that make up the country as well as domination by two colonial powers, Germany and Belgium. In spite of these political experiences and acts of ethnic violence, Rwanda remains a country with rich history, culture, and customs. Much has been written about the genocide of 1994, and more books continue to be published on the subject, but that regrettable episode is not the subject matter of this book. Rather, the book examines the culture and customs of Rwanda from earliest times to the present. It is an attempt to reveal some facts about the rich and interesting aspects of Rwandan culture and customs, which are often hidden from readers. Instead of focusing on the negative occurrences, this book presents the positive things to learn from Rwanda and its people. This book does not, however, claim to be a comprehensive exposition of the Rwandan culture and customs, but it does serve as an introductory study upon which further research can be conducted.

Acknowledgments

Shortly after the tragic 1994 Rwandan genocide came to an end, I was invited to make a presentation on Rwanda at Brookdale Community College in New Jersey. Although my knowledge of Rwandan history was limited, I accepted the invitation and presented a paper on the subject, which provided me with an opportunity to learn about and understand the ethnic and political situations in Rwanda and later became a springboard for this book. After reading the paper, Professor Toyin Falola invited me, on behalf of Greenwood Press, to write a book on the culture and customs of Rwanda. On account of my narrow understanding of this subject matter, I accepted reluctantly and faced the challenge. For his invitation and his strong support throughout this process, I want to thank Professor Falola. His guidance and suggestions helped me tremendously. I also want to thank Greenwood Press for giving me the opportunity to make this contribution toward widening the knowledge we have about a very small but important African country.

I thank Ms. Wendi Schnaufer, my first editor, who read and made suggestions on the outline and the first chapter. I also am indebted to Kaitlin Ciarmiello, my second editor, who read and corrected the entire manuscript. Kaitlin, I thank you for all your helpful suggestions.

Many people assisted me at the research stage. I am thankful to Dr. Eleazar Ziherambere of the American Baptist Churches in Valley Forge, Pennsylvania, for giving me his time to read part of the manuscript and for providing me with useful materials. I thank Dr. Pierre-Damien Mvuyekure of the Department of English Language and Literature at the University of Northern

Iowa for showing great interest in the project and for offering suggestions. I thank Mrs. Venantie Uwishyaka for the information provided and Mr. Buziz Claver for sending materials from Rwanda.

I received a lot of help from Monmouth University. My profound gratitude goes to Linda Silverstein and Sherri Xie of the Interlibrary Loan Department of Monmouth University Library for their great assistance in finding books and articles. To Robert Grasso, who helped in collecting materials and in proofreading the entire manuscript, I say many thanks. Bob provided invaluable service in making this book readable. I am grateful to Professor Saliba Sarsar, who always advised and encouraged me to complete the project. I thank all members of the Department of History and Anthropology for their support and understanding while I was writing this book. I cannot thank Dr. Funso Afolayan of the University of New Hampshire enough for his consistent encouragement and guidance.

I passed through a difficult time while writing this book, especially losing five close relations and friends in the span of three months. Combining teaching and official administrative duties also made the pace of writing this book very slow, but the inspiration and the vigor I received from Esther, my wife, and our children, Dorcas, Ruth, Emmanuel, and Rebecca, made it possible to persevere and complete the work. My family endured my inability to engage in some fun activities with them because of my writing project.

It has been fascinating reading and writing about Rwanda. Although Rwanda shares many similar aspects of culture and customs with the rest of sub-Saharan Africa, it also has its own unique society and culture. For the opportunity to investigate and write about the people of Rwanda, I thank them.

Although every attempt has been made to present a simple and accurate picture of Rwandan culture and customs, language barriers may have caused some misinterpretations or in-depth explanation. None of my sources were responsible for any inaccuracies that may be found; therefore, I accept responsibilities for the interpretations and flaws in this book.

Abbreviations

APROMOSA	Association pour la Promotion Sociale de la Masse (Association for the Social Promotion of the Masses)
CAURWA	Communauté des Autochtones Rwandais
CDR	Coalition pour la Défense de la République
ESAF	Enhanced Structural Adjustment Facility
FAR	Forces Armées Rwandaises
FAWERWA	Forum for African Women Educationalists, Rwanda Chapter
GDP	Gross Domestic Product
IDP	Ideal Democratic Party
IMF	International Monetary Fund
MSM	Mouvement Social Muhutu (Hutu Social Movement)
OAU	Organization of African Unity
PARMEHUTU	Parti du Mouvement de l'Emancipation Hutu
PDI	Democratic Islamic Party
RADER	Ressemblement Démocratique Rwandais (Rwandese Democratic Union)

RPF	Rwandan Patriotic Front
RTLM	Radio et Television Libres des Mille Collines
UNAMIR	United Nations Assistance Mission to Rwanda
UNAR	Union Nationale Rwandaise (Rwandese National Union)
UNHCR	United Nations High Commissioner for Refugees
UNO	United Nations Organization
VOA	Voice of America
WAMY	World Assembly of Muslim Youth
WCC	World Council of Churches

Chronology

1889	A solar eclipse of the sun occurs.
1894	German explorer Count von Gotzen arrives in Rwanda.
1896	German occupation begins and a military post is established at Shangi.
1899	Ruanda-Urundi is incorporated into German East Africa. Germany establishes colonial rule.
	The White Fathers arrive at Usumbura and establish the first mission station.
1902–1903	Famine occurs in Butare as a result of a widespread drought.
1911	German forces suppress a revolt organized by northern Hutu chiefs in reaction to their loss of political autonomy.
1916	Belgium takes over Rwanda from Germany. Belgium uses Tutsi traditional rulers to govern.
1922	The League of Nations puts Ruanda-Urundi under the trusteeship of Belgium.
1923	The Belgian authorities abolish domestic slavery by freeing Tutsi-held slaves.

1929   The Belgians make a number of colonial reforms.

1930   Belgian policy of forced labor begins, using the Tutsi chiefs to enforce it.

1931   The Belgians depose King Musinga and replace him with his son Rudahigwa.

            Christian Missionary Society (CMS) establishes a hospital at Kigeme.

1932   The Catholic mission establishes *Kinyamateka* as the first newspaper at Kigali.

1933   The Belgians introduce ethnic-based identity cards.

1945   The United Nations (UN) gives Belgium trusteeship over Rwanda.

            The Catholic mission begins the publication of *L'Ami,* a periodical.

1952   The colonial government creates a Tutsi-dominated Superior Council.

1954   Belgian authorities abolish *ubuhake.*

1957   A Hutu groups publishes the "Note on the Social Aspect of the Racial Problem in Rwanda," which is considered the manifesto of the Bahutu because it condemns the feudal system and the Tutsi hegemony.

1958   There is an increase in ethnic tension.

1959   The Hutu Social Revolution occurs. Supported by the Roman Catholic Church, the Hutu take power, and approximately 20,000 Tutsi die as others go into exile.

            King Mutara Rudahigwa dies under mysterious circumstances.

            Union National Rwandaise (UNAR) is formed.

1960   PARMEHUTU wins an overwhelming majority in the first municipal elections.

1961   King Kigeri V dies. PARMEHUTU proclaims Rwanda a republic, abolishes the monarchy by referendum, and wins parliamentary elections.

1962	Belgium grants independence to Rwanda. Grégoire Kayibanda is elected president and forms an all-Hutu government.
1963	Approximately 20,000 Tutsi are killed, and Tutsi refugees from Burundi, called *inyenzi,* organize an attack on Rwanda.
1964	The government establishes the Office des Cultures Industrielles du Rwanda (OCIR).
1966	The Rwandan franc is devalued.
1973	In response to Tutsi killing about 200,000 Hutu in Burundi, the Public Salvation Committees begin killing the Tutsi. Juvénal Habyarimana, chief of staff of the armed forces, takes power from Kayibanda in a bloodless coup. The 1962 constitution is suspended.
	The Office Rwandaise du Tourisme et des Parcs Nationaux is established in Kigali.
1978	A new constitution is formed, providing for a single-party system with the National Revolutionary Movement for Development (NRMD) as the state party.
1979	Rwanda National Union (RANU) is formed.
1987	The Rwandan Patriotic Front (RPF) is formed in Uganda.
1990	Pope John Paul II visits Rwanda. *Kinyamateka* journalists are tried. Habyarimana suppresses ethnicity on identity cards. The RPF attacks Rwanda. Belgium and France evacuate their nationals from Rwanda.
1991	Between 500 and 1,000 Tutsi pastoralists in Bagogwe are massacred. Rwanda returns to a multiparty system.
1992	The government declares a state of emergency in the Bugesera region, where ethnic violence, looting, and killing occur. The government signs a cease-fire agreement with the RPF in Addis Ababa, Ethiopia, and signs an accord in Arusha, Tanzania.
1993	The RPF launches attacks in the north. Another cease-fire is signed in Dar es Salaam, Tanzania. The Arusha

Peace Accords are signed. The UN deploys the United Nations Assistance Mission for Rwanda (UNAMIR) to Kigali. The RPF continues attacks.

1994   President Habyarimana of Rwanda and President Cyprien Ntariyamira of Burundi die in a plane crash. The genocide begins. The RPF captures Kigali and declares the end of the war. Pasteur Bizimingu becomes president.

1995   The UN Security Council recommends the arrest of people suspected to be involved in the Rwandan genocide. The UN Tribunal for Rwanda (UNTR) indicts eight suspects and charges them with crimes against humanity.

1996   Trials begin for Hutus involved in the 1994 genocide. Tanzania closes refugee camps and repatriates approximately 1 million Rwandans.

1997   Five human rights observers are killed in an ambush in Cyangugu, and the UN withdraws all human rights observers in Cyangugu, Kibuye, and Gisenyi to Kigali for security reasons. Frodouald Karamina, leader of a Hutu extremist political movement who coined the slogan "Hutu Power," is sentenced to death for his involvement in the genocide.

1998   U.S. President Bill Clinton visits Rwanda and apologizes for the U.S. lack of action in stopping the genocide.

2000   Elections are held, President Pasteur Bizimunga resigns, and President Paul Kagame is inaugurated.

2001   Rwandans elect 256,300 *gacaca* magistrates. Rwanda changes its flag and national anthem to reflect a new era of unity and reconciliation.

2002   The *gacaca* court system is officially launched. Presidents Joseph Kabila of the Democratic Republic of the Congo and Paul Kagame of Rwanda sign the Pretoria Peace Accord. In April, former President Pasteur Bizimunga is arrested for illegal political activities.

2003   Paul Kagame appeals for international support for Rwanda during the time of transition and preparations for presidential and parliamentary elections. On August 25, Rwandans go to the polls for the presidential election in the first multiparty election since independence. Paul Kagame wins overwhelmingly, and the RPF wins a landslide victory in the parliamentary elections.

2004   Pasteur Bizimunga, former president, is sentenced to 15 years in jail for embezzlement and inciting violence.

2005   Some 36,000 genocide prisoners are released to decongest the prisons.

2006   The government makes administrative changes by replacing the 12 provinces with smaller, ethnically diverse regions.

1

Introduction

A lush green world filled by dramatic mountains that tumble and twist as they roll across Central Africa ... a land where the colours seem brighter than in other places. It's true, Rwanda is beautiful.

—James Bowyer, *Footprint Magazine,* June 2000

LOCATION AND GEOGRAPHY

Rwanda is located in east-central Africa, in the Great Lakes region. Stretching from latitude 1°04′ to 2°50′ south and from longitude 28°50′ to 30°53′ east, it shares boundaries with Uganda to the north, Burundi to the south, Tanzania to the east, and the Democratic Republic of the Congo to the west. The Akanyaru River separates Rwanda from its sister state, Burundi.

Covering an area of 10,169 square miles, Rwanda contains many geographic features, such as the Virunga and Karisimbi Mountains where the altitude rises to nearly five thousand feet above sea level and declines from west to east. In the northwest are the volcanic Birunga Mountains, and gorillas can be found at the slopes of the Karisimbi and Nyaragongo volcanoes. With its location only two degrees below the equator, Rwanda enjoys a temperate climate because of its high elevation. During the two rainy seasons (February to May and September to December), heavy downpours usually occur daily. With an annual rainfall of approximately 30 inches, the western and northwestern parts of Rwanda receive more rain than the eastern section, whereas the southeastern part has a desert like terrain. The two dry seasons are January to February and June to August.

Rwanda agriculture and settlements in the hills. Mary Jelliffe/Art Directors & Trip Photo Library.

Numerous lakes, rivers, and volcanoes exist in Rwanda. Among the lakes are Burera, Ihema, Kivu, Mugasera, Muhazi, and Ruhondo. Lake Kivu, which is the largest and the most spectacular, drains into Lake Tanganyika. The most important rivers include the Doma, Mulembwe, Ndahangwa, and Rusizi. The Virunga Range, the major volcanic highlands, is found to the north of Lake Kivu on the borders of Zaire, Rwanda, and Uganda. Adding to Rwanda's natural beauty are animals such as buffalo, elephants, gorillas, hippopotamuses, lions, and zebras. Several varieties of gazelle, snakes, and fish inhabit Rwanda.

LAND

Rwanda has different vegetation zones. Although most of the country is savanna grassland, the western mountain ridge falls within the forest region, whereas the eastern section is characterized by wooded savanna. Continually expanding farming and cattle economies have led to deforestation and periodic droughts. Without access to the ocean, Rwanda is landlocked, but a sizable part of the land is fertile and suitable for farming and cattle rearing.

The main agricultural product is coffee, but other products include beans, peas, sorghum, maize (corn), banana, cotton, and tobacco. In spite of fertile land and flourishing agriculture, Rwanda's economy remains poor partly due to a lack of important mineral resources. Deforestation and the ever-increasing population create problems of land distribution and use. Furthermore, the mountainous areas prevent communication, industrial development, and commercial incentives. In these areas, infrastructure such as roads and railways are grossly lacking or inefficient.

POPULATION

Rwanda is a densely populated country. In 1900, Rwanda recorded a population of 2 million inhabitants. The population had risen to 2.3 million in 1956, but by 1978 the figure had further increased to 4.8 million. It rose to approximately 6.5 million in 1986, 7.1 million in 1991, 8.1 million in the last census in 2002, and the estimated figure for 2003 was 8.4 million. Ruhengeri Province is the most populous, whereas Umutara is the least populated area. With a land area of 10,169 square miles, the population density is around 819 persons per square mile, the highest in Africa. In spite of the 1994 genocide, the population remains high. The poor economy of the country does not correspond with the growth in population.

Overpopulation has been partly responsible for a series of demographic movements either to urban centers for employment purposes or to neighboring countries such as Burundi, Uganda, and Zaire (now the Democratic Republic of the Congo). Approximately 94 percent of the population lives in rural areas, earning incomes as farmers and cattle herders. The increase in both human and cattle populations poses a major problem for the government.

Nyanza (also known as Nyabisindu), located in the Butare Province, used to be the capital of the Kingdom of Rwanda, but the seat of power has shifted to Kigali, one of the largest cities in Rwanda. Kigali was founded in 1907 during the period of German colonial rule, and it became the center of power in 1962 when Rwanda gained independence from Belgium. Kigali has developed into an economic center for Rwanda. It is experiencing modernity and Western influence. Other towns include Butare, Gisenyi, Kibuye, and Ruhengeri.

LANGUAGE

Kinyarwanda and French are the official languages, although Kiswahili is spoken as a commercial language. Widely spoken by approximately 7 million people (Hutu and Tutsi), Kinyarwanda is a tonal Bantu language that belongs to the central branch of the Niger-Congo language family.[1] It has dialects such as Kinyabwisha and Kinyamulenge, and it is close to Kirundi, which is spoken in Burundi. Since the end of the genocide, English has become a growing language, gradually displacing French. Government officials speak English, newspapers are published in English, and English is taught in schools.

ETHNIC GROUPS

Unlike other countries in Africa that have many ethnic groups, there are only three in Rwanda. These include the Hutu, with about 84 percent of the population, the Tutsi (15%), and the Twa (1%). The Twa (Pygmy) hunters and potters are considered the indigenous people. The Hutu and Tutsi who migrated to the region at different times met the Twa in situ. Three things have differentiated these ethnic groups: occupation, social status, and physical features. The Tutsi as cattle owners are usually tall and slender, whereas the Hutu farmers are short and square. The Tutsi retain the exclusive right to own cattle, and for this reason the Belgians described Rwanda as a caste society. The groups share close cultural similarities, but it is more difficult to distinguish a Hutu from a Tutsi than the two from the Twa. No last names differentiate the Hutu from the Tutsi. Married women do not adopt their husband's last name, and children do not take the name of their parents. By the nineteenth century, when the Europeans arrived in Rwanda, the Hutu and Tutsi were identified not only by ethnic differentiation but also by marriage, occupational status, and politics.

THE HUTU

The origins of the Hutu are not clear, but they migrated from the north to present-day Rwanda circa A.D. 1000, mixing with the indigenous Twa people. They are Bantu-speaking farmers whose sociopolitical structure was based on the clan. The *abahinza* were clan heads who acted as kings. They were known as "those who cause things to grow" because they were believed to possess the power to cause rain as well as protect crops from insects and cattle from disease. As the first migrant group, the Hutu claimed ownership of the land, which they used extensively for farming. Both women and men participated almost equally in farmwork.

The people from the south of Rwanda refer to the Hutu collectively as Kiga, but the Hutu cattle herders in the northwest are called Hima. Due to their nomadic way of life, the Hima were not involved in politics. Because of their farming occupation, the majority of the Hutu population lived in rural areas.

The Hutu responded both to Tutsi political domination and to European colonization. They received Western education, were politically conscious, and became the first core of politicians in the early part of the postcolonial period.

THE TUTSI

The Tutsi, a warrior and Nilotic cattle-owning people, migrated to Rwanda between the fifteenth and sixteenth centuries from Uganda and occupied the Virunga region. Owing to their military experience, the Tutsi were able to subdue the Hutu and the Twa and assume political leadership. The Tutsi believed that they were destined to establish a political hegemony over the Hutu. Their belief was sustained by a legend that their descendants came from "the north" (heaven), bringing with them cattle, fire, and iron, which were instruments of power and wealth. Under the leadership of Gilhanga (Founder), the Tutsi settled in the land between Lake Muhazi and Lake Mugesera. The Tutsi achieved political and economic dominance in central Rwanda, founded kingdoms, owned cattle, and established the Abanyiginya dynasty during the time of Kanyaruanda (Gilhanga's son) who became the first *mwami* (king). Over several centuries, their kingdom expanded to cover most of the area occupied by modern-day Rwanda. An interlocking relationship emerged as the Tutsi became culturally mixed with the Hutu. Intermarriage occurred between the two groups.

Ownership of cattle became a symbol of prestige for the Tutsi. They evolved the political institution of the *mwami* as a sacred king and used royal drums as symbols of power and authority. The *mwami* was regarded as the source of life and symbolized unity for the Rwandan kingdom. Unlike the *abahinza* of the Hutu, the *mwami* held and wielded strong and wide political powers over both the Hutu and the Tutsi. To demonstrate his supremacy, the *mwami* controlled and distributed land. Three types of chiefs assisted and advised the *mwami* in performing his political duties: the military chief, whose responsibility was to defend and expand the kingdom; the cattle chief, who was in charge of grazing and settling disputes; and the land chief, who oversaw agricultural land and produce. Although the Tutsi politically dominated the Hutu, they were partly assimilated into the Hutu culture and language (Kinyarwanda). Before the Abanyiginya dynasty came to an end in 1961, when Rwanda became a republic, wealth, political power, and prestige rested firmly in Tutsi hands.

THE TWA

The Twa, a Pygmy people, were the original inhabitants of Rwanda who lived off the land as hunters and gatherers in the northern regions of the

Virunga Mountains. Their material culture was poor, and as nomadic people, they showed no signs of iron technology. Archaeological artifacts reveal only the use of animal and plant materials such as horns, bones, and skins. The Twa lived in symbiosis with the Hutu, who introduced them to iron tools and pottery. Twa potters are scattered in different parts of the country. When the Hutu and Tutsi arrived and utilized the land for farming and grazing, the Twa were pushed farther into the forests.

Unlike the Hutu and Tutsi, the Twa did not establish any strong relationship with other ethnic groups other than serving as singers and dancers. They have been unable to make significant contributions to the political and economic growth of Rwanda because of their small population, economic poverty, and the prejudice against them. Their culture and customs as well as their political, economic, and social structures were not as advanced as those of the Hutu and Tutsi.

In the 1994 genocide, the Twa also were killed. Since the recovery process began, there have been efforts to bring the Twa together so they can take their place in the political, economic, and social life of Rwanda. They are participating in the reconstruction and reconciliation process.

LIVING TOGETHER

Living together in harmony has been part of the Rwandan society, and traditional values supported a culture of peace. A proverb in Kinyarwanda says, *Aho ubuhoro buri umuhoro urogosha* (Where there is peace, a machete could cut the hair). Although the Hutu, Tutsi, and Twa pursued different occupations, their symbiotic relationship facilitated the political and economic structure of the society. They developed a complex and sophisticated society, speaking the same language and observing common religious belief systems. The Tutsi learned the Hutu Bantu language. As loyalty to the Hutu lineage of leaders gave way to Tutsi political power in the eighteenth century, Rwanda assumed a new political outlook, reaching the height of its power under powerful *mwamis* such as Mutara II (reigned 1830–1860) and Kigeri IV (reigned 1860–1895).

POLITICAL ORGANIZATION

Not much is known about the political structure of Rwanda before the Tutsi dynastic founders arrived. Small Hutu kingdoms existed in the northwest, in the modern-day provinces of Ruhengeri and Gisenyi. The Hutu *abahinza* rainmakers acted as rulers, but they were not invested with strong political powers. With the arrival of the Tutsi, the system changed to a monarchy. The monarchical system was a widespread political arrangement in precolonial African societies.

Rwanda's political structure was hierarchical. At the top was the *mwami* (sacred king), believed to have come from heaven. He was a source of life and symbol of unity for the nation. Like other African monarchs, the *mwami* held absolute political and military powers. Because the king derived his powers from the gods, his subjects were forbidden from revolting against him. Among the paraphernalia of the king was the *kalinga* (sacred drum), which was decorated with the testicles of slain enemies. As symbols of royal power, the *kalinga* was accorded the same respect as the king. The king surrounded himself with the *ubwiru* (royal ritualists), who performed complex religious rituals in order to consolidate his power. The *ubwiru* was a council of religious hereditary experts established presumably by the first *mwami* not only to perform regular rituals but also to serve as religious and political advisors to the king. They were kingmakers, responsible for naming and installing the new king. Like other chiefs, the *ubwiru* owned land as a source of revenue.

By reducing the Hutu lineage heads to mere land or hill chiefs with the primary responsibilities of collecting tribute and taxes for the *mwami,* the Tutsi had redistributed power and undertaken a restructuring of the political system. Access to political offices and economic resources became the prerogative of the Tutsi. Through the use of the military, Tutsi kings were able to expand their frontiers, particularly to the west.

Next to the king were different groups of chiefs: the *mutwale wa buttaka,* chief of the landholders, who was in charge of agricultural products; the *mutwale wa ingabo,* chief of men responsible for recruiting soldiers for the king; and the *mutwale wa inka,* chief of the shepherds who pastured over the grazing lands. These chiefs collected tribute for the king from the district subchiefs and from the *umusozi* (hill or mountain) chiefs. Most of the chiefs were Tutsi and were loyal to the *mwami.* Military chiefs also protected the frontiers and expanded the kingdom through military campaigns.

A semifeudal system evolved. As often occurred between pastoralists and agriculturalists, the Tutsi instituted a client relationship with the Hutu. The Tutsi provided cattle and military protection in return for Hutu service. Under the *mwami*'s control and the clientage system, a network of interlocking roles gave Rwandan society a measure of cohesion and political stability.[2]

The Rwandan kingdom reached the peak of its political expansion during the reign of Kigeri IV. To consolidate Tutsi control and cope with continuous warfare, Kigeri reorganized the army and conquered all the independent Hutu states. He was the embodiment of conquest and modernization. Establishing trade relations with the Swahili city-states along the coast, Kigeri was able to obtain firearms with which he equipped his army. The first European entered Kigeri's court in 1894. Succession disputes occurred after his death, and European colonization began during the reign of his son, Yuhi IV (1896–1931). In order to maintain a firm grip on his people, Yuhi IV collaborated with the German colonial powers.

EDUCATION

Education is an integral part of any society because it is one of the vehicles by which the culture and customs of the people are transmitted. Before the European Christian missionaries introduced Western education, Rwandans received a pragmatic traditional education. Fathers provided vocational training, such as farming, carpentry, commerce, and sculpture, to their sons, and girls were taught by their mothers how to clean house, fetch water, and assist in other domestic chores. In Rwanda, as in many other African societies, education for girls was restricted because of the notion that they would become only wives and mothers. It is important to note, however, that as wives and mothers, women perform an equally significant and essential role as conveyors of culture and customs, which can only be aided by a sound traditional or Western education.

Traditional Rwandan education emphasized the principles of dignity, diligence, discipline, mutual respect, and tolerance. Basketry, pottery, and weaving were also part of the educational curriculum. Storytelling was central in informal education because it was geared toward improving a child's ability or skill of expression. The combination of moral and vocational learning served to support the community. For example, André Sibomana points out that "it is forbidden to drink alcohol while you are sculpting because every movement must be precise and the craftsman must retain complete self-control. Mistakes are not allowed. Should the sculptor miss a stroke, he will either waste wood or injure himself."[3]

The Society of Missionaries of Africa (White Fathers), under the auspices of the Catholic mission, introduced Christianity and promoted religious education with a curriculum centering on prayer, love, and respect for other people. For many years, only the Roman Catholic Church provided and controlled elementary and secondary education. A minor seminary was available for those who wanted to train as priests or teachers. Becoming a devout Christian was encouraged. Although parents did not have the opportunity to obtain a formal education for themselves, they recognized its value and sent their children to receive Western education. Investing in education was a risk but a venture that many parents were willing to take.

The Belgian colonial government subsidized the cost of education. Going from elementary to secondary school or to the seminary was considered a path toward achieving a good education. Rwandans were taught the French culture and language. Several institutions now provide higher education. One of these institutions is the Le Grand Seminaire, established in 1936 for the training of priests. The National University of Rwanda (NUR), with campuses in Butare and Ruhengeri, provides mainly education in the humanities, although it offers courses in medicine and engineering. Many students receive university education from overseas schools, particularly in Belgium, France, and Germany.

In 1962, the government instituted free and compulsory primary education for children between the ages of 7 and 12. The system was disrupted in 1994 during the ethnic conflict. Since then, there has been no free elementary and secondary education, and the chances for higher education have been extremely limited, which explains why the level of illiteracy has been high. Overall, the level of literacy is 52.7 percent (51.6% for men and 44.8% for women). Before the genocide of 1994, the Rwandan educational system was moving toward providing a more functional technical education, but low enrollment for high school, the lack of systematic planning, and the poor economy made the attempt difficult to accomplish. Schools were understaffed and poorly equipped with materials to aid teaching. With the refugees returning home after the genocide, more difficulties were encountered: school buildings had been destroyed and there was an acute shortage of teachers. The regional variations in the educational system have left some areas marginalized, therefore educationally disadvantaged.

A transition from the use of French to English as the medium of instruction is under way. Although the government is trying to support education, the Forum for African Women Educationalists, Rwanda Chapter (FAWERWA) supplements by providing scholarships to promote education as a rebuilding tool for Rwanda.

ECONOMY, RESOURCES, AND TRADE

As an agricultural and pastoral society, the Rwandan economy revolved around land and cattle. The Hutu were the main food producers, using intensive labor with the hoe *(isuka),* machete or scythe *(umuhoro),* and the billhook as implements, producing a variety of food crops. They also were specialized ironworkers who produced and repaired farming, hunting, and fishing tools and manufactured weapons. Tutsi kings used the iron hammer and anvil, produced by the Hutu, as part of their royal regalia. Archaeological excavations indicate that the tomb of Cyirima Rujugira, a seventeenth-century *mwami,* contained two forged anvil hammers used as headrests.[4]

An economic symbiotic relationship existed between the Hutu and the Tutsi. Although the Hutu produced food crops, the Tutsi provided cattle and milk. By custom, the king claimed ownership of the land and could allow his clients to use it. The king's clients often acquired their own clients. To further implement their dominant position, the Tutsi instituted the feudal system or the patron-client relationship called *ubuhake. Ubuhake* was a form of forced labor on the part of the Hutu because they served the Tutsi aristocracy and could not own cattle but could herd for their patrons. The client did more than take care of his patron's cattle: He repaired the house and served in the military. This economic arrangement made it impossible for the Hutu to accumulate wealth, resulting in their economic depression and social oppression.

Herding, hunting, and fishing constituted integral and important aspects of the economic culture of the Rwandan people. The Tutsi pastoralists controlled the highest social status partly because of the wealth they derived from owing cattle and the *ubuhake* contract gave them dominant economic power over the Hutu. Caring for and milking the cattle were the responsibilities of the Hutu clients, but the Tutsi patrons enjoyed the nourishing milk and butter. The Hutu farmers supplemented their cultivation with raising goats and sheep but ensured that the animals did not destroy their farmland. In eastern Rwanda, the Banyaremera kept cattle, goats, and sheep. Among the Banyaremera, cattle were used primarily for economic reasons, for marriage transactions, and for sealing feudal relationships.[5] Over centuries of herding, livestock emerged as an indispensable part of the economic and social life of the society.

With a limited knowledge of farming, the Twa survived mainly by hunting, using instruments such as bows, javelins, spears, and traps. Living in the forest and mountain regions, their hunting vocation must have been determined by environmental factors. The Twa have been significantly marginalized economically and socially because they did not own land, but a variety of humorous lyrics, music, and dance, which are often blithely performed, demonstrate their hunting tradition. Among northern Hutu and Twa, beekeeping was practiced because bees produced honey that was "used to brew hydromel, the favorite drink of prominent Tutsi."[6] In modern times, poaching has become a problem in Rwanda, and to prevent this, the Nyungwe National Park in southwestern Rwanda was established as a forest reserve in 1933. The Rwandan government, working in collaboration with environmentalists, is trying to conserve the animals, especially the gorillas.

Surrounded by lakes and rivers, Rwandans engaged in fishing to supplement farming, especially in Lake Kivu in the west and Lake Muhazi in the east. Commercial fishing is carried out by fishermen using small canoes and nets to catch tilapia.[7] Fishing remains an underdeveloped sector of the economy, but the government's attempt to restructure it should offer incentives to fishermen and yield more revenue.

Some other industries that enriched Rwandan economic culture included basketry, making of gourd containers, metalwork, painting, pottery, and wood carving (carving mainly religious or traditional images). The basket industry traditionally has been dominated by women, who use leaves found high in the mountains or low in the swampy areas. Baskets were used for both personal and religious purposes and were designed to contain liquids, especially milk used in rituals.

The Twa not only specialized in hunting, they also mastered the use of clay and became professional potters. The Urewe pottery, which characterized the expansion of the Bantu-speaking peoples, was found in Rwanda. The makers of the Urewe pottery presumably interacted with and influenced the Twa potters. Like the Tutsi who composed songs and dances to glorify their warrior tradition, the Twa celebrated their pottery culture with music and dance. The growing pottery industry and the need for international trade led to the creation of the Pottery Project by the Communauté des Autochtones Rwandais (CAURWA), the national nongovernmental organization for the Twa.

The spread of iron metallurgy produced significant results on the economy and social life of the people. The knowledge of iron smelting by the Hutu led to the emergence of specialized ironworkers who not only forged but also repaired farming, fishing, and hunting implements as well as weapons. Smithing evolved as a hereditary vocation and so-called smith kings were created. Besides serving an economic purpose, metalwork also was connected with politics and religion because iron hammers and anvils formed part of the Tutsi's symbols for royal authority. Archaeological excavations of the graves of Cyirima Rujugira and Kigeri Rwabugiri indicated that there was an interconnectedness of iron and rituals. Whereas the income derived from these industries was relatively small, it supported the household and helped sustain the local economy. The art and skills for these industries have been passed on from generation to generation.

RESOURCES

Rwanda has consistently faced economic problems arising from its agriculture-based economy, underdeveloped resources, and a lack of industrialization and technology. The government has been faced with deforestation and soil erosion problems because much of the land is utilized for the cultivation of coffee and tea. A significant reduction in Rwanda's annual earnings occurred when the world price of coffee fell in the 1980s. The main natural resources are gold, hydropower, methane, and tin ore.

Since the end of the genocide in 1994, the Rwandan government has made impressive improvements in rebuilding, rehabilitating, and stabilizing its social and economic infrastructure. Continued international aid and the strengthening of world coffee and tea prices led to economic growth. Attempts have been made to curb inflation and reduce the poverty level. Both rural and urban economic expansion is taking place. For example, Rwanda began a privatization program and signed an agreement with the International Monetary Fund (IMF) for an Enhanced Structural Adjustment Facility (ESAF) in 1998. Although agriculture made up 40 percent of the gross domestic product (GDP) in 2001, manufacturing (focusing mainly on the processing of agricultural products) contributed about 20 percent of GDP. Coffee and tea production has been unable to support the growing economy.

TRADE

Internal and external trade arrangements existed as an integral part of the economy before the colonial period. Informal networks through family ties and friends facilitated short-distance trading. The primary articles of exchange were food crops traded at local markets. Trading by barter was practiced, but before the introduction of currency, hoes were also an acceptable medium of exchange.

The Kinyagans in the southwest established a network of regional trade with central Rwanda,[8] involving the exchange of food crops for articles such as beads, bracelets, hoes, mats, livestock, especially goats, salt, and tobacco. The most important item of trade was the ornamental *ubutega* (anklet or bracelet), with which women adorned themselves. Rwandans traded with Egyptian merchants who penetrated the Great Lake region and with Arabs and Swahili-speaking merchants along the eastern coast.

The Europeans introduced the cultivation of cash crops, thereby altering the trade pattern in Rwanda. The Germans and the Belgians turned Rwanda into a primary producer of coffee and tea. In this trade relation, European currency was used, and cash rather than cattle became a symbol of wealth. Colonialism made international trade possible, especially with Rwanda producing coffee and tea. Today, the currency is the Rwandan franc, and because of the unstable economy, the exchange rate has been weak.

FOOD AND DIET

Operating in a subsistence economy, Rwandans grew and consumed mainly staple food crops. Their diet comprised mainly bananas, beans, corn, millet, peas, sweet potatoes, cassava, and fruits such as avocados, mangos, and papaya. They also ate vegetables such as spinach. A majority of the people ate twice a day, having sweet potatoes and porridge mixed with milk for breakfast and boiled beans, bananas, sweet potatoes, or cassava for lunch. Other foods included *umutsima* (a dish of corn pasta), *isombe* (cassava leaves), and *mizuzu* (fried plantains). Believed to have been introduced by the Germans and Belgian missionaries, potatoes became an important part of the Rwandan diet.[9] Potatoes can be eaten fresh or dried and are cultivated on a large scale in Gitarama and Butare.

Variations occurred in the Rwandan pattern of eating. In spite of their intensive labor, the Hutu did not eat on regular basis and consumed less meat and milk. The Tutsi ate even less food and drank more milk. In addition, only the Tutsi ate mutton, and their ownership of cattle enabled them to eat a more balanced diet than others. Among the Twa, only children were permitted to eat eggs.

Rwandans have experienced numerous health problems, essentially because of a lack of protein in their diet. Unlike in the urban centers where beef and chicken were consumed, people in the rural areas did not eat meat or drink milk on a regular basis. This was because cattle (seen as a sign of wealth and status) were not often slaughtered for meat. Fish, especially tilapia, were eaten by those close to rivers.

Beer was consumed in social and religious activities such as marriages and divination rituals. As hospitable people, Rwandans offer beer to their guests. Drunkenness was commonplace, and the Hutu even have songs for beer drinking.[10] Through a process of fermentation, men brewed an alcoholic drink made out of dry sorghum known as *ikigage* (may also have medicinal powers) and *urwagwa* (a kind of traditional banana beer). Although women seldom drink alcohol, men frequently drink beer with straws from a single large container.

A traditional Rwandan practice of collective work is called *ubudehe,* which portrays a sense of unity, collectiveness, and togetherness primarily for economic purposes. *Ubudehe* was an inclusive practice by members of the rural society in terms of gender and social status and involved the digging of fields before the rains and the planting and harvesting of crops. Because the system had always been useful and effective, the government revived it to serve "as a model for a program designed to alleviate poverty and provide for community rebuilding in the wake of the Rwandan genocide and civil war in the early 1990s."[11]

CULTURAL ISSUES

Housing Pattern

A large percentage of the Rwandan population inhabited rural areas in simple shelters. Their houses were mainly beehive-shaped huts with members of the same lineage living together in a circular enclosure or compound, which was surrounded by banana plantations. On vacant plots of land around the huts were planted crops such as beans, corn, and sorghum. Wealth determined the beauty and size of the house, and because of their privileged political and economic positions, the Tutsi owned large and well-decorated homes.

Clothing

A society's clothing pattern is often determined by factors such as climate, culture, marital status, religion, and wealth. Because of the warm climate, Rwandans did not wear heavy clothing. Traditionally, Hutu men wore goat-skins and bark shirts, the Twa wore skins from antelopes, sheep, or goats, whereas the Tutsi wore cow, leopard, or lion skins. It was not uncommon to find Hutu girls wearing belts of either lion or leopard skin, but as a mark of wealth, importance, and ethnic distinction, Tutsi girls wore belts of lion's or leopard's skin with fringes. Women also wore ornamental jewelry and rings. The importation of brightly colored clothes from Arab and Persian merchants along the eastern coast of Africa enriched the clothing patterns of the Rwandan people.

The impact of colonization has been far-reaching on the clothing pattern. Since independence, successive governments have encouraged the use of imported clothes from the Western world. A textile industry, established in Kigali, has been producing tons of various kinds of cloths on an annual basis. Rwandan tailors make different styles of pants, shorts, and shirts.

SOCIAL ORGANIZATION

Operating on a patrilineal system, the Rwandan society had the *inzu* (hut or household) as the core of kinship relations. An *inzu* consists of a husband, wife, and children (the nuclear family) in addition to close relatives (the extended family). The man maintains a strong influence as head and unifier of the family. Another kinship unit known as *umuryango* (lineage) and headed by the *umukungu,* the oldest and most influential male, consists of people from a number of households who have traced their descent to a common male ancestor. The *umukungu* wields influence because he has riches and is able to feed his family. His functions include the settling of disputes for family members and representing the family in political matters. Members of the family and the lineage live together in compounds in a close-knit family relationship; respect for one another is promoted even while lighthearted joking occurs between relatives of alternate generations.

Marriage within each ethnic group was common, but there has been extensive Hutu-Tutsi intermarriage. Because of the difference in social status, more Tutsi males marry Hutu women than Hutu males marry Tutsi women. When a Hutu man married a Tutsi woman, his social status was raised. As in other African societies, a Rwandan man paid a bride-price, such as a cow, to the bride's father before the marriage was consummated. The purpose of the bride-price was to legitimize the marriage, but it was returned if the marriage ended in divorce. Due to a lack of money to pay the bride-price and a shortage of land to set up a new household, men often delayed marriage.

Child training was part of the family's responsibility. The child goes through a training period in order to learn oral traditions, respect, hard work, and the appreciation of Rwandan culture and customs. Several social activities were organized to bring together boys and girls. Social values and self-expression were encouraged, especially in storytelling.

RELIGION

As in other parts of Africa, Rwanda was a polytheistic society, with religion serving as a unifying force. The people have the concept of a supreme being whom they call Imana. Imana is conceived as the creator and preserver of life, and his power transcends that of the lesser spirits. Popular religious cults were the Ryangombe, Nyabingi, and Kubandwa (to grab). Adherents who are initiated into the Ryangombe cult are called *imandwa* (the ones who are grabbed). The *imandwa* have been grabbed by Ryangombe, the lord of the spirits. This cult was possibly of Hutu origin.

A belief in life after death and ancestral worship were prevalent. A dead person transformed into *abazimu* (the spirits of the dead) but continued to be involved in human matters. They were considered honored, sacred, and venerated spirits. Family members consult them and communicate with them through an *umupfumu* (diviner). If not regularly and appropriately propitiated, it was believed that the *abazimu* could cause disaster, sickness, or crop failure. As a measure of prevention, Rwandans consulted an *umupfumu* to explain why the *abazimu* were angry and to ask what they could do to pacify them. Although Ryangombe was the most powerful ancestral spirit, Nyabingi was venerated as a female spirit in northern Rwanda.

The people of Rwanda also revere animal totems. Among many African societies, animal, plant, and reptile totems were a sociocultural phenomenon. What is revered or how it is revered varies from place to place. Totems were created for clans or individuals. Some clans not only regarded the animals portrayed on their totems as their ancestors, they also adopted their names. The spread of animal or plant totems may be the result of migration.

In Rwanda, the Abazigaba clan is associated with the leopard, the Abega clan with the frog, and the Abagesera with the wagtail. The members of these clans were prohibited from killing or eating the animals symbolized on their totems. Some animals were even given a human burial if found dead. Unlike other totemic societies, the Rwandan clans did not believe that they descended from an animal or that the animals embodied the souls of their ancestors.

Christianity was introduced to Rwanda in the late nineteenth century by the European missionaries, especially the Roman Catholic missionaries (White Fathers). Led by the Roman Catholic Church, a rapid spread of Christianity occurred in Rwanda. Education and health care were used to gain converts. Today, Rwanda is predominantly Roman Catholic. Approximately 65.5 percent of the Rwandan population is Roman Catholic, 26 percent Protestant, and 11.1 percent Adventist. Accusations that the Catholic Church and its priests were supportive of the 1994 genocide caused a recent acceleration in the number of converts to Islam.

COLONIALISM

Though the European imperial rule over Africa began in the second half of the nineteenth century, Count von Gotzen, the first European to arrive in Rwanda, did not do so until 1891. The terrain had prevented the Arab slave dealers from entering the interior. During the partition of Africa in the 1890s, Rwanda became a German colony as part of German East Africa. After establishing a military station in Kigali in 1907, effective German colonial control began in 1910 with Richard Kandt as the first colonial resident governor. The Germans adopted the indirect rule system and increased Tutsi influence for three reasons: for the convenience of their administration, for the continuation of a traditional inexpensive structure of power that suited their economic exigencies, and for their belief in the Tutsi being ethnically superior to the Hutu.

In 1918, after World War I, control over Rwanda was mandated to Belgium. Like the Germans, the Belgians intensified and institutionalized Tutsi authority over the Hutu and Twa. They gave full support to the authority of the *mwami* and his chiefs. They systematically denied the Hutu positions of authority, claiming that only the Tutsi could be officials. The Hutu also were denied higher education in secular schools but could study in religious seminaries. In addition, the Belgians issued identity cards to underscore and formalize ethnic differentiation. By perpetrating a divide-and-rule policy, the Belgians had prepared the way for a revolution. The encouragement and intensification of ethnic division and patronage forced the Hutu to look for redress, knowing that they were exploited and repressed. The Hutu demanded that the Belgian government terminate all anti-Huti discriminatory policies, which included educational, employment, and political privileges given to the Tutsi.

Nationalist activities began in Rwanda, as in the rest of Africa, after World War II. By the 1950s, the Belgians gradually began to listen to the voices of the Hutu elite with a view toward promoting a democratic system in a divided society. Realizing that the Belgian colonial government had begun to show more favor to the Hutu by encouraging power sharing, the Tutsi not only embraced the principles and process of decolonization but also pushed hard for independence. They sought international support, especially from communist countries—an action that further weakened their relationship with Belgium. The Hutu elite wanted a delay of independence to give them more time to prepare, gain concessions from the colonial authority, participate in preindependence politics, and perform leadership roles. The Parti du Mouvement de l'Emancipation Hutu (Party of the Movement for the Emancipation of the Hutu, PARMEHUTU) became a strong organ of the Hutu that advocated for power from the colonial authority.

THE 1959 SOCIAL REVOLUTION

The preindependence tension continued until 1959 as both groups mass-mobilized to the extent that a trivial issue had the potential to ignite violence. Such hostility erupted in 1959. On July 24, 1959, King Mutara III died under mysterious circumstances. Shortly thereafter, Kigeri V was installed as king, resulting in a mass rebellion of Hutu. Although the genesis of the conflict (popularly known as the Hutu Social Revolution) was in long-standing social inequality, political deprivation, and pervasive rural grievances, the Hutu goal was to terminate Tutsi dominance. Fueling the crisis was the clash between members of two rival political parties: PARMEHUTU and the Union Nationale Rwandaise (Rwandese National Union, UNAR). A Hutu subchief, Dominique Mbonyumutara, was allegedly attacked, beaten, and killed by the youth wing of UNAR. Reacting to the rumor, the Hutu and moderate Tutsi from the Ressemblement Démocratique Rwandais (Rwandese Democratic Union, RADER) began to burn Tutsi houses and destroy Tutsi properties. During the revolution, many Tutsi were killed, whereas others, including the king, went into exile in neighboring countries. In a 1961 referendum, the monarchy was abolished, and the Hutu consolidated their political power by establishing a republic.

INDEPENDENCE MOVEMENTS

The process of decolonization, which took place all over Africa after World War II, had a significant effect on the development of nationalist movements in Rwanda. Ethnically affiliated political parties were formed in the 1950s. Grégoire Kayibanda formed the first political party, the Mouvement Social Muhutu (Hutu Social Movement, MSM), in June 1957. The party focused on economic, political, and social reforms. In November 1957, a Hutu businessman, Joseph Gitera, founded the Association pour la Promotion Sociale de la Masse (Association for the Social Promotion of the Masses, APROMOSA) with its stronghold in the Butare area. Gitera used the party's newspaper, *Ijwi rya rubanda rugafi* (The Voice of the Common People), to challenge the privileges that the Tutsi enjoyed and to demand independence for Rwanda. In response to the growing Hutu nationalist movement, the conservative Tutsi formed UNAR in August 1959. UNAR was essentially a promonarchy and anti-Belgian military party. In September 1959, Chief Prosper Bwanakweri, a Tutsi moderate, formed RADER to counter the activities of the conservative UNAR.

Grégoire Kayibanda was one of the leading nationalists. Educated in Roman Catholic schools, Kayibanda served as a teacher and an information officer for the Belgian colonial government. Strongly in favor of Hutu domination, Kayibanda openly and strongly campaigned for Hutu rights in 1957. He and other Hutu leaders unsuccessfully put pressure on the Belgian government to delay independence until the Hutu were ready to assume the political leadership of the country. Kayibanda had studied in Belgium and after his return to Rwanda reorganized the Mouvement Social Muhutu, turning it into a strong political party, and renaming it Parti du Mouvement de l'Emancipation Hutu (PARMEHUTU). He used the *Kinyamateka* newspaper, of which he was the editor in chief, to promote Hutu interest and Rwandan independence.

Hutu nationalist activities were directed at both the Belgian colonial powers and the dominant Tutsi group. Nationalist activities were increased by both ethnic groups in spite of the Belgian administration prohibition on political meetings in order to avoid ethnic conflict. Following the death of King Mutara III in 1959, a Hutu social revolution broke out in which the new king, Kigeri V, was forced into exile in Kenya. The revolution was a liberation movement for the Hutu as reflected in the results of the first national elections held in June 1960. PARMEHUTU convincingly won, and Kayibanda became the prime minister. In a continuing effort to consolidate Hutu political power, Kayibanda organized a referendum in September 1960, which officially abolished the Tutsi monarchy, and he declared himself executive president. During the first two years of his regime, the Tutsi in exile, led by *inyenzi* (cockroaches; this word took a new meaning during the genocide) guerillas, undertook a number of raids.

POSTINDEPENDENCE PERIOD

The 1960s was a decade of independence throughout Africa. Feeling the winds of political change, the Belgians granted independence to Rwanda in 1962. Political power transferred from the Belgians to the Hutu. Under the Hutu administration, the privileges, which the Tutsi enjoyed during the colonial era, were eliminated, and a system of institutionalized segregation emerged. Divisiveness, which had plagued Rwanda throughout its history, continued for years after independence.

The Tutsi went on the offensive to fight the Hutu dictatorship. Those Tutsi who had gone into exile as a result of the 1959 Hutu social revolution attempted to stage a comeback, but their forces were driven back in 1963. In the encounter, the Hutu killed approximately 10,000 and sent another 150,000 into exile. Kayibanda remained firmly in control and his reelection as president in 1965 and 1969 proved his popularity among the Hutu.

In the early 1970s, Kayibanda's popularity began to decline for two reasons. First, his government faced economic problems, and second, he appointed some educated Tutsi to government positions, thereby removing the political opportunities and privileges granted to his Hutu constituents. Supported by moderate Hutu, the Tutsi who had gone into exile formed the Rwandan Patriotic Front (RPF), and their efforts to reclaim power culminated in a bloodless military coup led by Juvenal Habyarimana in May 1973.

THE ARUSHA PEACE ACCORDS

Following a protracted period of conflicts, unrest, and insecurity, peace-making talks were held between the Rwandan government and the RPF. Sponsored by President Ali Hassan Mwiniyi of Tanzania and launched on July 10, 1992, the peace talks were intended to promote dialogue, seek conflict resolution, and evolve a sustainable peace. Tanzanian Ambassador Ami Mpungwe facilitated the talks.

Participants came from within and outside Africa. They included representatives from the government of Rwanda and the PRF, delegates from six African countries (Burundi, Nigeria, Senegal, Uganda, Zaire, and Zimbabwe), and representatives from the Organization of African Unity (OAU), United Nations Organization (UNO), Germany, and Belgium. The first round of talks called for a cease-fire, and subsequent ones focused on reconciliation, power sharing, political cooperation, security, and the issue of refugees. Although the power of the president was considerably reduced, the transitional broad-based government (TBBG), which included the RPF and the Rwandan government, was empowered to form a coalition government.

Not willing to share power with the PRF, the Coalition pour la Défense de la République (Coalition for the Defense of the Republic, CDR) initially opposed these arrangements and refused to sign the agreement. Later, the PRF also refused to sign, and the situation remained unsettled until the genocide began in 1994. The Arusha Accords were signed on August 4, 1993, but could not be implemented because of the continuing ethnic tension. Overall, the Arusha peace negotiation failed to accomplish some of its overall objectives. Detailing the issues that led to the failure of the Arusha Accords and the subsequent Tutsi genocide, Gilbert Khadiagala argued that "The Arusha Accords will go down in history as one of the most dismal failures of international diplomacy."[12]

The Hutu and loyalists to Habyarimana saw the failure of the accord as a betrayal and began to find strategies to deal with the ethnopolitical situation. By March 1994, an elaborate plan had been made to kill Tutsi politicians and educated Hutu who opposed Habyarimana's regime.

As one of the measures to bring peace, the Arusha Peace Accords in 1993 amended the Rwanda constitution of 1991. Additionally, new constitutions were adopted in 1995 and 2003. In order to avoid future conflicts, the 2003 constitution, which was overwhelmingly ratified by referendum, focused on democracy and equal representation for the Hutu and Tutsi as the two main ethnic groups but also took cognizance of the historically marginalized Twa and women. President Paul Kagame believes that because "Rwanda has experienced a long period of bad governance and the women and Batwa have been the main victims of this unhappy history,"[13] positive steps should be taken in the new constitution to be in their favor so that they would have a sense of belonging and be duly represented.

THE GENOCIDE OF 1994

Genocide, the deliberate and systematic killing of a cultural, ethnic, or racial group, has existed since ancient times. Genocide may be caused by a loss of power by a particular group, unhealthy interethnic or interracial rivalry, or merely a natural dislike for a group of people. Raphäel Lemkin, a Polish-Jewish scholar, first used the word in 1944 to describe the conspiracy of the Nazis in Germany to wipe out the Jews. In 1948, the United Nations (UN) declared genocide an international crime and condemned it. Article II of the UN Convention on the Punishment and Prevention of the Crime of Genocide states:

> In the present convention, genocide means any of the following acts commit-
> ted with intent to destroy, whole or in part, a national, ethnical, racial or religious

group, as such: (a) Killing members of the group; (b) Causing serious bodily or mental harm to members of the group; (c) Deliberately inflicting on the group conditions of life calculated to bring about its physical destruction in whole or in part; (d) Imposing measures intended to prevent births within the group; (e) Forcibly transferring children of the group to another.[14]

Genocide may have ideological, retributive, economic, or political underpinnings. It is an immoral, criminal, and conspiratorial act that violates the rules of humanity. Alain Destexhe described genocide as "both the gravest and the greatest of the crimes against humanity."[15] It is a heinous crime because it not only leads to insecurity and mistrust but also destroys and obstructs progressive political, social, and economic programs. It slows the process of nation building.

Aside from the Jewish Holocaust, other acts of genocide during the twentieth century include the massacre of Armenians by the Turks in 1915, the killing of approximately 2 million Cambodians by the Communist Khmer Rouge between 1975 and 1979, the killing of thousands of Indians in Guatemala by the national army (1981–1983), and the massacre of Bosnian Muslims by Serbian forces in 1991. Although there may be exceptions, it appears that genocide often occurs in a nondemocratic society.

Women and children at Nyakaraui transit camp. Howard Sayer/Art Directors & Trip Photo Library.

As mentioned previously, the Hutu-Tutsi interethnic rivalry has a long history. The devastation resulting from this contention is incalculable. None of the previous conflicts, however, compared in magnitude with that of 1994, which was triggered by the death of President Juvenal Habyarimana (a Hutu) and his Burundi counterpart Cyprien Ntaryamira in a plane crash on April 6, 1994. Habyarimana and Ntaryamira were returning from Tanzania, where they had gone to negotiate the timetable for the implementation of the Arusha peace talks. Alleging that the plane was shot down by the Tutsi-dominated RPF, the Forces Armées Rwanda-ises (FAR) of the Hutu reacted by a mass killing of the Tutsi. The killers called themselves *interahamwe* (those who attack together), and radio propaganda was used to recruit more Hutu. The Tutsi also went on the offensive, killing the Hutu, turning the conflict into a war between the FAR and PRF. Between April and July 1994, approximately 800,000 Hutu and Tutsi had been massacred, thousands had been maimed, and millions had become refugees in Burundi, Tanzania, Uganda, and Zaire. Killed along with Tutsi were moderate Hutu such as Agatha Uwilinguy-imana (prime minister) and Joseph Kavaruganda (president of the Supreme Court). Because of the violence unleashed by the *interahamwe,* Elizabeth Neuffer indicated that, "no one was safe, not women, not chil-dren, not the elderly, not priests, not nuns."[16] A climate of fear descended on the whole country; the lives of all Hutu, Tutsi, and Twa were in jeopardy.

The world community did not immediately respond to the deteriorat-ing situation in Rwanda in spite of the reports of atrocious genocide. For example, the United Nations Assistance Mission to Rwanda (UNAMIR), a multinational force of 5,000 troops under the command of Canadian Lt. Gen. Romeo Dallaire, was stationed in Kigali but was withdrawn when the genocide began. The Belgian government also withdrew its forces. The United States government under President Bill Clinton did not support the UN sending a large force to restore peace in Rwanda. Reporting to the Security Council of the UN on May 31, 1994, Secretary-General Boutros Boutros-Ghali stated, "We have failed in our response to the agony of Rwanda, and thus we have acquiesced in the continued loss of human lives.... There can be little doubt [that the killing in Rwanda] constitutes genocide."[17]

To take care of the refugees, estimated at about 2 million, the United Nations High Commission for Refugees (UNHCR) maintained refugee camps, where shelter, food, clean water, health facilities, and other essential services were provided.

Tutsi refugees in transit in Rwanda. Howard Sayer/Art Directors & Trip Photo Library.

RWANDA SINCE 1994

Rwandans claim that there was no ethnic conflict in the precolonial times. If disputes occurred, cultural traditions and mechanisms were used to quickly restore peace. For example, the Kubandwa cult could be consulted and elders could be called upon to settle disputes. Rwanda was ravaged by the ethnic conflict of 1994 and its people are still dealing with the reality and magnitude of the genocide. The government is faced with the difficult and challenging task of bringing together a war-torn country and an ethnically divided people. The concept of *gacaca* (traditional court system that promotes peaceful living together) has to be applied in the rebuilding process. The *gacaca,* as practiced by the people of Rwanda, is a democratic system of justice in which the judges and people sit in the open air on the grass to judge cases.

Many Rwandans believe that they can overcome the genocide, trust each other again, and live together peacefully. The idea of solving ethnic rivalry by creating a Hutuland and Tutsiland is frowned upon, because such did not exist and should not exist. Creating two separate lands would promote continued divisiveness, competition, and unrest. Living together again will help in the healing process, will provide a profound opportunity for nation building, and will foster social harmony.

The government has embarked on reconciliation, reconstruction, and rebuilding programs with assistance from the world community. Living together after the devastation of genocide requires a bold step from the government and a significant amount of sacrifice on the part of the people. The depth of the mistrust, fear, and hatred makes it difficult for an immediate and quick solution; it has to be a long-term process. More than ten years after the genocide, efforts continue to determine how to bring peace and stability to Rwanda and to prevent future nightmares.

NOTES

1. Francis Jouannet, ed., *Kinyarwanda, langue Bantu du Rwanda* (Paris: Société d'Études Linguistigues de France, 1983); Alexandre Kimenyi, *A Relational Grammar of Kinyarwanda* (Berkeley and Los Angeles: University of California Press, 1980); Alexandre Kimenyi, *A Tonal Grammar of Kinyarwanda* (New York: E. Mellen Press, 2002).

2. René Lemarchand, "Power and Stratification in Rwanda: A Reconsideration," in *Peoples and Cultures of Africa,* ed. Elliot P. Skinner (New York: Natural History Press, 1973), 416.

3. André Sibomana, *Hope for Rwanda: Conversation with Laure Guilbert and Hervé Deguine* (London: Pluto Press, 1997), 4.

4. F. L. Van Noten, "The Iron Age in the North and East," in *The Archaeology of Central Africa,* ed. F. L. Van Noten (Graz, Austria: Akademische Druck-und Verlags-anstalt, 1982), 69–76.

5. Pierre Bettez Gravel, *Remera: A Community in Eastern Ruanda* (The Hague, Netherlands: Mouton, 1968), 93.

6. Marcel d'Hertefelt, "The Rwanda of Rwanda," in *Peoples of Africa,* ed. James L. Gibbs Jr. (New York: Holt, Rinehart and Winston, 1965), 411.

7. Richard F. Nyrop, Lyle E. Brenneman, Roy V. Hibbs, Charlene A. James, Susan MacKnight, and Gordon C. McDonald, *Rwanda: A Country Study* (Washington, DC: United States Government, 1982), 164.

8. David Newbury, "Lake Kivu Regional Trade in the Nineteenth Century," *Journal des Africanistes* 50, no. 2 (1980): 6–36.

9. G. Durr, *Potato Production and Utilization in Rwanda* (Lima, Peru: International Potato Center, 1983).

10. Alan P. Merriam, *African Music in Perspective* (New York: Garland, 1982), 68.

11. Judith Dunbar, "Ubudehe and the Kecamatan Development Projects: Case Study and Comparative Analysis" (master's thesis, Tufts University, 2004); République Rwandaise, Ministère des Finances et de la Planification Economique, *Ubudehe mu Kurwanya Ubukene* (Kigali, Rwanda: Ministry of Finance and Economic Planning, April 2, 2003).

12. Gilbert Khadiagala, "Implementing the Arusha Peace Agreement on Rwanda," in *Ending Civil Wars: The Implementation of Peace Agreements,* ed. Donald S. Rothchild and Stephen John Stedman (Boulder, CO: Lynne Rienner, 2002).

13. "Batwa: Rwandan President to appoint Minorities in Senate," *UNPO,* http://www.unpo.org/article.php?id=1207, September 24, 2004.

14. United Nations General Assembly, "Convention on the Prevention and Punishment of the Crime of Genocide," December 9, 1948, Human Rights Web, http://www.hrweb.org/legal/genocide.html.

15. Alain Destexhe, *Rwanda and Genocide in the Twentieth Century* (New York: New York University Press, 1994), 4.

16. Elizabeth Neuffer, *The Key to My Neighbor's House: Seeking Justice in Bosnia and Rwanda* (New York: Picador, 2001), 248.

17. Stephen D. Wrage, "Genocide in Rwanda: Draft Case Study for Teaching Ethics and International Affairs," paper presented at the International Studies Association, Los Angeles, California, March 14–18, 2000, http://www.ciaonet.org/isa/wrs01.

2

Religion and Worldview

Africans are notoriously religious, and each people has its own religious system with a set of beliefs and practices. Religion permeates into all the departments of life so fully that it is not easy or possible always to isolate it.

—John S. Mbiti

Religion has always occupied an important place in the culture and customs of the Rwandan people. Prior to and during the colonial period, religion was central to the people's political, economic, and social life; it formed the foundation of their culture and customs. The Rwandan people fell within the typology of traditional worshippers before the introduction of Islam and Christianity. Sacred objects, persons, places, and natural phenomena were revered. Ceremonies and rituals were performed on a regular basis to appease gods or ancestors. Individuals as well as clans held life and religion as sacred. Religion was real to Rwandans because it was a part of every aspect of their lives from birth to marriage to work to illness to death. Rwandans believed that religion also could provide insight into the future.

WORLDVIEW

The people of Rwanda, like their other African counterparts, are deeply religious; unlike other counterparts, they do not have an intricate hierarchy of gods and goddesses. Because the Hutu are of the Bantu origin, their worldviews are similar to those other Bantu groups. They hold a concept of the supreme being and interpret almost every event or occurrence from a religious

Some families built shrines for their ancestors to house them and acknowledge their importance. Ancestral spirits were considered sacred and were to be venerated. Family members communicated with their ancestors through an *umupfumu* (witch doctor). If not regularly and appropriately propitiated, it was believed that the ancestors could become malevolent, causing disaster, sickness, misfortune, or crop failure. To stop or prevent such mishaps, Rwandans consulted the witch doctor to explain why the ancestors were angry and to ask what they could do to pacify them.

Ryangombe (of Hutu origin) and Nyabingi are the most powerful and celebrated ancestral spirits. Ryangombe was a culture hero and a warrior who died in a strange circumstance. Tradition claims that a buffalo hit him with its horns and threw him to a special tree called the *umurinzi*. When attempting to get up, all the trees around wanted to hold him, but it was the *umurinzi* that held him up until he died. The tree became so important that at every special occasion, people must hold the leaves of the tree.[6]

Ryangombe founded the cult in order that people would honor him at death.[7] Initiation into the Ryangombe cult means officially recognizing the authority of Ryangombe over oneself. Although Ryangombe was celebrated mostly in southern and western Rwanda, Nyabingi was venerated as a fertility goddess in northern Rwanda. For the Nyabingi cult, there are no initiation rites, but there are priests and priestess.[8]

One of the more popular religious cults among the Hutu was the Kubandwa, meaning "to grab" or "to get initiated," and whose leader was Ryangombe and the adherents are called *imandwa* (the ones who are grabbed). Grabbed by Ryangombe, the lord of the spirits, the *imandwa* have become his lieutenants. During the celebration, Hutu peasants acted as if possessed and performed rituals as a symbolic protest against Tutsi dominance. The *imandwa* were found mostly in southern Rwanda, where they held an elaborate and expensive process of initiation rituals.

A common cultural and religious practice was the formation of alliances based on blood relationships, called *kunywana* (meaning "to cut and drink blood"). It was a bond of brotherhood with the purpose of establishing and strengthening family ties and friendship. The intent behind the practice was to create peaceful and friendly relationships, especially among children. The agreement also might include a stipulation not to reveal secrets of or report a crime performed by a brother. The *gacaca* traditional court recognized the blood relationship and would not force anyone to give testimony against a blood brother.

Although it was meant to be a lifelong pact, it could be broken, but if broken, it was believed that natural calamity, such as leprosy or sudden death, would befall the offender. Because the agreement could be made with men of different clans and ethnic groups, there were many Tutsi and Hutu blood brothers in central Rwanda. This practice helped bring up children to respect friendships and family relationships. Because this aspect of Rwandan culture involves blood, it has been discouraged. Family relationships remain strong, but the exchange of blood has been discontinued presumably because of the widespread cases of HIV/AIDS.

Divination was performed by diviners *(umupfumu)* who also acted as charm makers, ritual purifiers, or rainmakers. Both men and women were capable of being diviners. Diviners possessed the supernatural powers to talk to the ancestors as well as to know and interpret their wishes. Diviners were consulted for things such as success at work, peace in the community, appeasing the ancestors, and warding off evils or misfortunes. Family members could consult diviners to interpret the wishes of the ancestors in order to appease them. The diviners performed their functions by using various techniques and items such as a candle made from animal fat, chicks, sheep, or bull calves. The king had ritual specialists who resided in the royal court and performed divinations through the use of a bull calf. Converts to Christianity have to denounce this practice in accordance with the beliefs of the new religion.

The people of Rwanda believed that disease was caused by either physical or mystical reasons. This idea served to accentuate the belief in tangible and intangible things. To this end, traditional healers treat all kinds of diseases. Witchcraft was also a common practice as part of the people's indigenous religious beliefs. Witches are believed to be the causes of death, disaster, misfortune, and bad harvest by using all kinds of magical power. Because of their nefarious activities, people suspected of being witches or those who associate with them are often openly attacked. They could be excommunicated from the community, humiliated, or killed.

Medical practitioners or diviners *(abapfumu)* have the power to communicate with the spirits of the dead and to protect the living from malevolent acts from the dead ancestors or witches. The *abapfumu* use leaves, plants, and roots to make protective charms for their clients, and they receive pay for their services. Although some diviners are rainmakers, others engage in divination, healing or preventing diseases, interpreting dreams, and foretelling the future. In times of war, diviners provide protective medicines for soldiers. Given their spiritual power, the "special equipment and clothing—a gourd rattle, leopard-skin cape, and cowtail headdress" of the diviners are "considered sacred."[9] The skill and paraphernalia of office are passed to sons or young neophytes through an informal method.

Among many African societies, animal, plant, and reptile totems were a sociocultural phenomenon. What is revered or how it is revered varies from place to place. Totems were created for clans or individuals. Some clans not only regarded the animals portrayed on their totems as their ancestors, they also adopted their names. The spread of animal or plant totems may be the result of migration. In Rwanda, it is believed that both humans and animals are endowed with a spiritual force, but when an animal dies, the spiritual force vanishes. Clans were associated with one kind of animal or another. For example, the Abazigaba clan is associated with the leopard, the Abega clan with the frog, and the Abazirankende clan with the wagtail. The Baishekatwa clan of southern Rwanda was associated with the grasshopper.[10] The members of these clans were prohibited from killing or eating the animals symbolized on their totems, and they could not cut down their totem plant. Animal totems were even given a human burial if found dead. Unlike other totemic societies, the Rwandan clans did not believe that they descended from an animal or that animals embodied the souls of their ancestors.

CHRISTIANITY IN RWANDA

Rwandans experienced a series of political and socioeconomic crises before the European missionaries, especially the Roman Catholic missionaries, introduced Christianity in the late nineteenth century. On their arrival, Christian missionaries recognized the stratification and the powerful institution of kingship in Rwandan society. The missionaries attempted to understand the culture of the people, their traditional religious beliefs and practices, and the king who performed complex religious rituals through the *abiru* priests.

The European exploration into the interior of Africa in the late nineteenth century eventually opened Rwanda to the outside world. Explorers such as Richard Burton, J. H. Speke, and H. M. Stanley went close to Rwanda but did not enter the kingdom. The first European explorer to enter the kingdom of Rwanda was Count von Gotzen. Thereafter, Christian missionaries followed. Bishop Joseph Hirth (1854–1931) was a member of the Société des Missionaries d'Afrique (Society of the Missionaries of Africa, also known as the White Fathers). Cardinal Charles Martial Allemand Lavigerie founded the Society of the Missionaries of Africa in 1868 in Algiers (Algeria). Before Cardinal Lavigerie died in 1892, 278 Roman Catholic missionaries had traveled to different parts of Africa, including Rwanda. Operating from Uganda, Joseph Hirth was the founder of the Roman Catholic Church in Rwanda. Born in France, ordained a priest in 1878, and speaking fluent German, Joseph Hirth participated in the first expedition of the Catholic missionaries to Central Africa.

In the wake of military and political intrigues in Central Africa, Hirth proceeded slowly to Rwanda in 1899 and attempted to establish a religious, economic, and political relationship with King Yuhi Musinga. On the instructions of Cardinal Lavigerie, the Catholics in Rwanda devoted much of their time to the Tutsi ruling class on the erroneous assumption that the conversion of the king would result in the automatic conversion of his people. The initial alliance with the Tutsi rulers helped widen the gap between the Tutsi and Hutu ethnic groups.

The Germans had established their colonial rule in Rwanda three years before Hirth's arrival, and it was anticipated that working with the king and the Germans would facilitate the process of evangelizing the Rwandan people. In February 1900, Hirth opened the first Catholic mission at Save, northeast of Butare. German missionaries founded schools in which many Tutsi, but few Hutu children, were given Western education. The station in Save soon attracted many people, especially those Hutu who needed protection from their landlords. The ability of the missionaries to treat wounds and heal diseases also brought many sick people to the station. Apparently, sociopolitical circumstances drove the Hutu to embrace Christianity.

As Cardinal Lavigerie directed, the Catholic missionaries identified with the people's culture and customs by speaking their language, eating their food, and wearing Rwandan-made clothes. They performed catechism in the Kinyarwanda language, established seminary education, and emphasized priestly life.[11] Their practical approach through cultural and social interaction created a welcome and loving atmosphere and prepared the way for the flowering of Christianity. By April 1901, two more stations had been opened in Zaza (Gisaka Province) and Nyundo (Bugoyi Province).

Christianity was, however, growing in a hostile environment. First, laborers for the construction of mission stations were paid cheaply, making the Hutu converts and workers become hostile toward the missionaries. The Hutu basically worked for free because the missionaries often took permission from the king to use the Hutu as workforce. This was part of the policy of forced labor that the colonial powers adopted in Africa. Second, the initial close relationship with the Tutsi rulers prompted the Hutu converts to regard the missionaries as agents of political domination to be avoided. For example, "Rumours spread that children taken in for instruction were destined ultimately for the mwami, who would hand them over to Nyina'rupfu, Mother Death."[12] Third, clash of interests between the missionaries and the Tutsi rulers resulted in tense relations. Although the missionaries wanted to spread Christianity, the Tutsi rulers and nobles jealously guarded their economic interests, political positions, and social status. They did not want the white missionaries to displace them or to erode their traditional roles and power. Relations between King Musinga and the Catholic Church, which were initially friendly, later became hostile. Religious and political riots, especially in the Gisaka, Save, and Zaza regions, led Musinga to conclude that the missionaries were interfering too much in politics and in the local affairs of his people. To deal with the missionaries, Musinga turned to the Germans for help. In response, the Germans raided the Gisaka station, killing thirty people. That incident slowed missionary activities. Furthermore, the Tutsi became less enthusiastic about practicing Christianity and hostile because they considered the European missionaries as imperialists who were attempting to usurp their political power.

The fallout with the Tutsi rulers prompted the Catholic Church to collaborate with the German and Belgian colonial powers. This was a continuation of the search for political support in order to facilitate evangelization. Although the German colonial government favored the Tutsi for their administrative convenience, the Catholic Church began a vigorous effort to evangelize and educate the Hutu. For several decades when the Tutsi worked with the Germans to maintain their power, the Hutu became friendly with the missionaries, an attempt to emphasize their fundamental right of equality with the Tutsi. The lack of support from the Tutsi courts presumably accounted for the limited success of the Catholic missionaries. A strong Catholic-Hutu alliance was established, however, and the strategy became successful, especially in the rural areas. From the Catholic Church perspective, Christianity could serve to assist the marginalized Hutu in their social advancement.

The Catholic-Hutu alliance and the progress in educating the Hutu alarmed the Tutsi aristocracy, who began to convert starting from 1921. King Musinga was friendly to the missionaries and allowed them to operate in Rwanda because he needed their support to consolidate his position, being a usurper to the throne. As the Catholic Church grew in power, it was able to influence political decisions. For example, in 1931 the Catholic Church was instrumental in the deposition of King Musinga. Thereafter, a significant number of royal family members and their courtiers became Christians. This change of attitude by the Tutsi further helped the spread of Christianity.

Many Hutu not only converted but also took advantage of the Western education that the Catholic Church provided. They became catechists and were ordained as priests. For example, Grégoire Kayibanda, one of the foremost Rwandan nationalists, was a product of Catholic education.[13] He attended the seminary before proceeding to Belgium to study journalism. Additionally, the European missionaries studied and practiced the Rwandan culture and spoke the Kinyarwanda language while their converts spoke in their native languages. According to Elizabeth Isichei, "The first Rwanda catechism was a composite of pidgin kinyaRwanda, Rundi, and Swahili, and the first Rwanda seminarians studied in Latin, conversed in Swahili, and corresponded with their European counterparts in German."[14]

Later, Catholic advances continued to be successful under Belgian colonial support. The progress of the Hutu in Western education alarmed the Tutsi, who began to see Christianity and education as "alternative sources of prestige and authority."[15] Hence, there occurred an influx of Tutsi to the Catholic Church. In 1938, Alexis Kagame, a prominent Tutsi and court historian, became the editor of *Kinyamateka,* a Catholic newspaper that started publication in 1933. He was ordained a priest in 1941. With active and educated Hutu and Tutsi, Catholicism made significant inroads into the political and social life of the people. Further progress was made through native Rwandan priests who were engaged in converting their own people. As Isichei pointed out, "by 1948, there were 88 white Fathers, 81 Rwanda secular priests, 58 Rwandan teaching brothers, and 155 indigenous nuns in Rwanda."[16] The most significant development took place on October 27, 1946, when Mwami Mutara III converted to Christianity.

As part of its efforts to reach the people with its doctrines and spiritual teachings, the Catholic Church established a number of periodicals. For example, the *L'Ami* began to circulate in 1945, changing its name to *Temps Nouveaux* in 1955. *Kinyamateka* also circulated widely in the 1950s, serving as a vehicle of disseminating ideas, which were not or could not be expressed in other publications. The Grand Seminaire de Nyakibanda at Butare founded the *Urunana* paper in 1967, publishing three times a year. A monthly review called the *Dialogue,* edited by a Belgian priest, was founded in 1967.

The constitution of Rwanda allows freedom of religion, but Roman Catholicism has attracted more followers. By the 1990s, a large population of Rwandans had adopted Christianity. In the 1991 census, approximately 90 percent of the population was Christian (63% Roman Catholic, 19% Protestant, and 8% Adventist). Only a small community in Kigali and some urban centers of the country embraced Islam before 1994. The huge number of Christians suggests the extent to which Christianity has penetrated the cultural, political, and social life of the people of Rwanda. In spite of the growing number of Christian adherents, traditional religions endure in many parts of Rwanda. Syncretism (blending of religious beliefs) was common, especially in the rural areas.

CHRISTIANITY AND THE GENOCIDE

Ethnopolitical conflicts and social classification predated the introduction of Christianity in Rwanda. From the colonial period to postindependence, such conflicts were brought to the church's attention. The Catholic Church attempted to transform the society by preaching equality and unity. Given the magnitude and prevalence of divide in the traditional society, the message of brotherhood, equality, and unity had little impact on the people. The publication of the *Kinyamateka* newspaper, beginning in 1933, created political awareness and opened a forum for discussion on equality and unity. Christian missionaries applied the doctrine of no separation between the Greeks and the Jews to Rwandan society in order to teach equality between the Hutu and Tutsi, between the rulers and the ruled.

It was surprising that in spite of the number of adherents among the Rwandan people, Christianity was unable to prevent the outbreak of the genocide. To many people, the Catholic Church did not enjoy a good reputation because of its deep involvement in the country's ethnic and political affairs during and after the colonial period. An example is the Most Rev. André Perraudin, a White Father and bishop emeritus of Kabgayi, who lived in Rwanda for 38 years. Before he retired to Switzerland in 1993, some people demonstrated in front of his church in Kabgayi in Rwanda, accusing him of encouraging anti-Tutsi sentiments. This accusation was based on one of his publications in 1959 that called for democracy, justice, and social reforms.[17] Although Perraudin was calling for an ideal situation, the Tutsi aristocracy interpreted it as Catholic Church interference in internal politics and an attempt to eradicate the Rwandan monarchical system—that is, the Tutsi hegemony.

In the pre-1994 period, Rwanda "appeared to be a model of national piety, a profoundly Christian country, with high levels of church attendance among Catholics and Protestants."[18] Christianity was a popular and influential religion; it was more or less a state religion. The Catholic Church was, however, accused of playing a negative role in the genocide because it did not do enough to stop the killing, and it is alleged that some of its priests supported the massacres. Accusations surfaced that the parish priest at the Nyange Church in Western Rwanda ordered the church bulldozed on top of Tutsi refugees, resulting in the deaths of approximately 2,000 people. Various priests and nuns have been put on trial as further evidence of the Catholic Church's alleged involvement in the massive killing. Instead of supporting one group against the other or keeping silent, the Catholic Church should have spoken out and opposed the injustice in the society.

Looking back at the historical relationship between the Catholic Church and the Tutsi, there has always been that continuing accusation of racism against the church: the church favoring the Hutu over the Tutsi. The Hutu Manifesto of 1957, which led to the Hutu Social Revolution of 1959, was believed to have been connected with the church because Grégoire Kayibanda, the leader of the revolution, was a recipient of a Catholic education and the editor of the Catholic journal, *Kinyamateka*. As mentioned before, most of the Hutu elite were products of the educational system provided by the

Catholic Church. Many people saw the favoritism that came from the Catholic Church as a negation of its crusade for Rwandan unity. In a country where Christians are in the majority, it was expected that Christianity would be a strong force for peace.

It is, however, important to note that the history of Christianity in Rwanda has been that of shift in support. At different times, the Catholic Church enjoyed the support of the Tutsi, the colonial powers, and the Hutu. The close relationship between the Catholic Church and the Hutu administration was unfavorable to the Tutsi. In order for Christianity to adequately perform its social roles, no ethnic group should be favored at the expense of the other. According to David Gushee, the reinforcement of ethnocentric thought and the cozy relationship that the leaders of the Catholic and Protestant churches enjoyed, "weakened the church's ability to resist the quasi-fascist genocidal racism" of the Hutu.[19]

On the basis that Christians or the clergy who were decisively involved in the genocide acted on their individual capacities, the church failed to accept responsibility. The question is: Did the church actually have the ability and authority to stop the killings that emanated from such deep-rooted ethnic conflicts? What could the church do when Christians were killing fellow Christians? Christianity could not hold back the accumulation of heavy weapons and could not prevent outside forces that encouraged the genocide. The Christian Council of Rwanda made efforts to bring the people together, but the efforts were blocked by powerful forces. Not possessing the political authority and military power to intervene and restore peace limited the role of the church in the conflict. The underlying causes for and the resulting massacre went well beyond what the church could control.

CHRISTIANITY AFTER THE GENOCIDE

Although the role that the church played during the genocide has been heavily criticized, not much has been mentioned about the loss the church suffered. Approximately 300 priests and members of religious orders were killed.[20] Christianity, in particular, seemed to have lost some power and prestige as seen in some antichurch government policies. The Roman Catholic Church has been called upon to reevaluate its practices and policies that have encouraged ethnic divisions. Christians, whether Catholics of Protestants, helped in the process of resettling the refugees. One of the emerging public roles of Christianity in contemporary Rwandan political history is to be more forthcoming in promoting activities and policies that are geared toward ethnic and national unity.

Today, in order to ease the tension between the church, the government, and the people of Rwanda, support for the victims of the genocide has poured in from different Christian groups. Rwanda has witnessed a proliferation of religious faiths, each attempting to rebuild the society, to promote unity, and to teach religious tolerance. Christianity has come to the forefront in preaching forgiveness and reconciliation. Christian relief groups coordinate with nongovernmental organizations (NGOs) to provide for the survivors. Foreign missionaries propagate their religion as well as receive government support because of the development programs on which they embark. Even though the Catholic Church has received negative criticism, it is making efforts to maintain its position and to win back members, especially the youth, by organizing education, sports, and camping programs.

Christianity also has found its way into the prison system, where pastors are involved in the *gacaca* process by praying for and preparing the accused for hearings. *Gacaca* courts are one type of traditional court established to prosecute the perpetrators of the genocide. In the face of emergency and in search of justice, Rwandans decided to revive traditional customs. According to an inmate, "Pastors have come to do programs and explain about Gacaca. We are willing to be taught, but maybe it's already too late." During the genocide, "Everyone killed someone, and it was not a crime."[21] Because the damage to peaceful coexistence has been extensive, Christianity has tremendous work to do in the process of restoring the Hutu-Tutsi relationship. Although forgiveness and reconciliation are possible, it is hard for victims to forget their experiences.

Protestant and Evangelical churches, which were not found in the pre-genocide era, have been established and are thriving in Rwanda. Not associated with the genocide, the leaders of the new churches have drawn the attention of the people as well as the government. The new churches draw their membership from the Roman Catholic Church, and most of them receive funding from U.S. Christian organizations. Revivals are constantly organized for the purpose of restoring the confidence of the people in the church and helping in the overall healing process.

The Episcopal Church of Rwanda organized the Interfaith Commission for Re-integration of Rwanda. The commission is headed by both Christian and Muslim leaders. The World Council of Churches (WCC) has not been left behind in promoting healing programs and fostering unity in Rwanda. The WCC believes that Christianity has to play an important role in the transformation of the whole Rwandan society. Religion, particularly Christianity, is seen as a means to bring renewed hope and provide a strong and effective therapeutic for the survivors.

Islam

Islam, since its introduction by the Swahili Arab merchants who traded in ivory and slaves along the East African coast in the eighteenth century, has not been a widely practiced religion in Rwanda for two reasons. First, Rwanda-Swahili coastal contacts were more of a commercial than religious nature. Most of the Arabs who visited Rwanda were merchants rather than missionaries. King Kigeri IV (1860–1865) purchased muskets from the Muslim Swahili traders and did not convert to Islam or promote the religion. Second, Catholicism and Protestantism had gained tremendous ground, and the German colonial authorities favored Christianity over Islam. For many centuries, Islam flourished only among Muslim immigrants from neighboring regions such as Kenya, Sudan, Tanzania, and Uganda. Unlike other religions, Islam remained an urban religion because most of the immigrants settled in cities.

A viewpoint has been expressed that Islam arrived in Rwanda during the German colonial period. Because the Germans needed soldiers, clerks, administrative assistants, and merchants, they recruited Muslims from the Swahili-speaking coast of Tanzania to help forge a larger German East Africa. This did not, however, translate into the German promotion of Islam. Many of the first-generation Muslims married local Rwandan women, creating a tradition of interethnic marriages whose progeny would for a long time be regarded as foreign.[22]

The first mosque, the Al-Fatah Mosque, was constructed in 1913 during German colonial rule. Because the Germans did not promote Islam, the religion did not easily find an inroad among the indigenous people. Later under the Belgian administration, Islam still would not play a significant role in Rwanda. Unlike Christianity, which wielded influence and gained converts through education, Islam would not enjoy that advantage; the first Muslim school was not built until 1957. Although Rwandan authorities recognized Islam after independence in 1962, that was not enough to make it a popular religion. The Muslims, mostly of the Sunni branch of Islam, were found mostly in Kigali, especially in the Biryogo quarter where the Al-Fatah Mosque was located.

Because of the dominance of Christianity, especially the Roman Catholic Church, Islam did not grow and did not influence the politics of the country. The opportunity to grow presented itself as a result of the 1994 genocide in which some Catholic priests and Protestant clergy were accused of supporting and equipping the Hutu Interahamwe soldiers.[23] The role of Islam and Muslims in the genocide became a source of attraction, and many Rwandans converted. Thus, the religion, which had been on the periphery, suddenly soared in popularity and recognition. Mosques and Qur'anic schools now have been constructed in nearly all the major cities and towns, and the Friday prayers are usually well attended. At the Al-Aqsa Mosque in Kigali, worship services are held on a regular basis in which Rwandan Muslims are enjoined to faithfully practice the Five Pillars of Islam. Expressing the growth of Islam within the Rwandan population, a Muslim leader said, "We're everywhere."[24] From about 7 percent before the genocide, the Muslim population has increased to 14 percent since 1994.

To maintain and strengthen this newfound popularity, Muslim leaders emphasize peace, unity, reconciliation, and religious tolerance in their sermons. They teach about respect for one another and about brotherhood, proclaiming that Hutu and Tutsi are the same in the Islamic faith. Muslims go to the rural areas promising to provide education to the young ones. The attraction of education outside Rwanda is prompting the youth to accept Islam.

One Muslim leader has been quoted saying, "We have our own Jihad, and that is our war against ignorance between Hutu and Tutsi. It is our struggle to heal.... Our Jihad is to start respecting each other and living as Rwandans and as Muslims."[25] The mosque has provided a forum for Rwandans not only to worship but also to speak and express thoughts about their existence in order to find reconciliation and heal their wounds. The World Assembly of Muslim Youth (WAMY), established in Saudi Arabia in 1972 as an international independent organization, is a member of the United Nations Nongovernmental Organizations, which is helping to promote Islam in Rwanda. Islam is now taking an important part in the process of Rwandan reconciliation and reconstruction.

Along with the rest of the Muslim world, Rwandan Muslims observe Eid al-Fitr (a celebration that marks the end of Ramadan, the month of fasting) and Eid al-Adha (a celebration that honors the prophet Abraham) as public holidays. The observance of these holidays follows the lunar calendar.

OTHER RELIGIONS

The predominance of Christianity and the growing influence of Islam have overshadowed the presence of other religions such as Baha'i, Buddhism, and Hinduism, which are practiced primarily by foreigners, especially Asian businesspeople from Bangladesh, China, and India. The adherents of these religions are not aggressive in converting Rwandans. Hence, they exist in small communities of worshippers. For the religions to thrive in Rwanda and attract the indigenous people, they have to incorporate some aspects of the local culture. Unlike the commonly found churches and mosques, there are no places of worship for Buddhism and Hinduism. As minority groups, Buddhists and Hindus in Rwanda tend to be secretive. Faculty and students in higher institutions most likely practice these religions.

RELIGION AND POLITICS

For many centuries, religion was closely tied to political affairs in several parts of the world. Priests wielded influence because of their close association with the rulers. In Rwanda, the Tutsi maintained their political supremacy and their dynastic control over the people using military and religious powers. The interaction between religion and politics remained strong during the colonial period because the Germans and the Belgians did not stop the Tutsi rulers from performing their political and spiritual functions. A new dimension surfaced when the monarchy was abolished and a democratic form of governance was adopted.

The constitution of Rwanda guarantees freedom of religion, and successive governments have respected all religions in the country. Rwanda has no state religion, and the government has always tried to separate religion from politics. According to the constitution, all citizens of Rwanda have the freedom of association and freedom of religion. The constitution guarantees equality "without any discrimination, especially in respect to race, color, origin, ethnic background, clan, sex, opinion, religion, or social status."[26] In light of this provision, the Democratic Islamic Party (PDI) changed its name to the Ideal Democratic Party (IDP). The constitution does not prohibit religious instruction in schools. Hence, Christian and Muslim schools primarily reflect the denomination of their founders.

In recognition and respect for religions, the government does observe religious holidays. Christian holidays include Easter, Assumption Day, All Saints' Day, and Christmas, and Islamic holidays are the Eid al-Fitr and the Eid al-Adha.

It is not strange that religion was an integral part of the Rwandan political system in precolonial times; it happened throughout Africa. Religion was a source of political empowerment for rulers. As mentioned before, the king surrounded himself with the *abiru,* who performed complex religious rituals. Traditional religion was used to uphold political power. On their arrival, the Roman Catholic missionaries attempted to penetrate the Tutsi court, but the kings showed little interest and did not give any serious commitment. Because of this lack of interest, the missionaries directed their evangelical efforts to the Hutu rural population, among whom they had considerable success.

The period of German rule, which began in 1898, was terminated in 1917 when the Germans were expelled. The Belgians took over the colonial administration of Rwanda and gave the French-speaking missionaries special treatment. With this collaboration, religion and politics continued to go hand in hand in Rwanda. The Belgian colonial government adopted the indirect rule system, which increased the Tutsi's monopoly of political power.

The church endorsed the innate ability and superiority of the Tutsi along with the colonial policy of divide and rule, which left the Hutu all the more in a disadvantaged position. Additionally, the issuing of identification cards with ethnic classification in the 1930s further widened the gap between the Hutu and Tutsi. It limited the Hutus' participation in politics and made it difficult for the church to uphold the principle of equality and unity. The carrying of identification cards left a lasting and indelible mark on the social and political history of Rwanda.[27]

The religion and worldview of the people of Rwanda are intertwined with their political, economic, and social structures. Between the precolonial and colonial periods, the king was an embodiment of religion and power and maintained his position through a complex process of rituals. Depending on land and rain for cultivation, the king was expected to protect his people and the kingdom from droughts or floods and to control rainfall by performing regular religious rituals.

With the coming of Christianity and colonization, Rwanda went through rapid and intensive social change. Roman Catholicism gradually replaced indigenous religions for many, but others blend Christianity with traditional beliefs and practices. Protestant churches, and in more recent times evangelical churches, have overshadowed but have not completely displaced indigenous religions. The abolition of kingship also reduced religious rituals that formerly were performed by the rulers. A shift in political power from the Tutsi to the Hutu occurred through the support of the Belgian colonial administration and the Roman Catholic Church. The Hutu who benefited from Catholic education provided the core of political leadership at independence, but with the return of power to the Tutsi, there was evidence of a strained relationship between the government and the church.

The outbreak of the 1994 genocide did not help the growth and continued influence of Christianity, particularly the Roman Catholic Church. Years after the genocide, the Tutsi-led government adopted an antichurch policy based upon the role of the Catholic priests in the mass murder. The visit of Pope John Paul II in 1990, however, began a process of change in church-state relations. In spite of the criticisms against the church, Christianity is still growing, although its dominance is no longer in the hands of the Catholic Church. Protestant and evangelical churches are playing a very active role in the reconstruction of Rwandan society. Religions have to play their public roles in order to have a meaningful and successful democratic reconstruction of Rwanda. These roles include active participation in the peace and reconciliation process, openly denouncing ethnic marginalization, and supporting educational programs that inspire and prepare the youth who are future leaders of the country.

A new phenomenon has emerged in Rwanda with the efforts to make Rwanda the first so-called purpose-driven nation in Africa. Rick Warren, the author of *The Purpose-Driven Life* (2002), and his wife have received the attention of President Paul Kagame. Given the realities and the results of the genocide, the economic poverty, and low standard of living, Warren believes that his Christian ministry can help alleviate the suffering of the Rwandan people. There are questions to ask in regard to this new development. For example, how receptive of this new trend would the Rwandans be in view of the disillusionment they have experienced with Christianity? Although many people all over the world suggest that for democracy to work, religion must be separate from politics, how is it that Paul Kagame is embracing religion and bringing it into politics? He must believe that Christianity has a role to perform in changing Rwanda.

List of Some Churches in Rwanda

Anglican Church
Baha'i
Baptist Church
Church of the Nazarene
Episcopal Church of Rwanda
Evangelical Churches
Methodist Church
Jehovah's Witness
Pentecostal Churches
Presbyterian Church
Roman Catholic Church
Seventh-Day Adventist Church
Zion Temple Church

Notes

1. John S. Mbiti, *African Religions and Philosophy* (London: Heinemann, 1969), 39–42.

2. Ibid., 211.

3. Jan Vansina, *Antecedents to Modern Rwanda: The Nyiginya Kingdom* (Madison: University of Wisconsin Press, 2004), 57–58.

4. Christopher C. Taylor, *Milk, Honey and Money: Changing Concepts in Rwandan Healing* (Washington, DC: Smithsonian Institution Press, 1992), 33.

5. Jan Vansina, *L'évolution du royaume Rwanda des origins à 1900* (Brussels, Belgium: Academie Royal des Sciences d'Outre-Mer, 1962).

6. The worship of Ryangombe represents the Old Testament for Rwandan converts to Christianity. Instead of holding the *umurinzi* leaves, Christians hold cypress

fronds, which represent the New Testament. At Christmas, the cypress tree is widely used by Christians.

7. Lucy Mair, *African Societies* (London: Cambridge University Press, 1974), 175.

8. C. C. Taylor, "Rwandans," in *Worldmark Encyclopedia of Cultures and Daily Life,* ed. Timothy L. Gall (Farmington Hills, MI: Thomson Gale Publishers, 1997).

9. J. K. Pomeray, *Rwanda* (Philadelphia: Chelsea House, 2000), 76–77.

10. The Baishekatwa clan presumably migrated to southern Rwanda from the Bunyoro kingdom, where the grasshopper was a royal totem. Carole A. Buchanan, "Courts, Clans and Chronology in the Kitara Complex," in *Chronology, Migration and Drought in the Interlacustrine Africa,* ed. J. B. Webster (New York: Africana, 1979), 97–98.

11. Ian Linden and Jane Linden, *Church and Revolution in Rwanda* (New York: Holmes and Meier, 1977), 32–34.

12. Ibid., 35.

13. Ibid., 289.

14. Elizabeth Isichei, *A History of Christianity in Africa* (Lawrenceville, NJ: Africa World Press, 1995), 133.

15. Ibid., 247.

16. Ibid.

17. The pastoral letter for Lent, published on February 11, 1959, read, "The divine law of justice and social charity *(charité)* requires that the institutions of a country be structured in such a way that they ensure for all legitimate social groups the same fundamental rights and the same opportunities for human advancement as well as participation in public affairs. Institutions approving of a regime of privileges, favouritism and protection, be it for individuals or for social groups would be at odds with Christianity." Helmut Strizek, *Human Rights in Rwanda: Life after Genocide* (Aachen, Germany: Missio, Human Rights Office, 2003), 10.

18. Stephen D. Smith, "Introduction," in *Genocide in Rwanda: Complicity of the Churches,* ed. Carol Rittner, John K. Roth, and Wendy Whitworth (St. Paul, MN: Paragon House, 2004), 1.

19. David P. Gushee, "Why Churches Were Complicit: Confessions of a Broken-Hearted Christian," in *Genocide in Rwanda,* ed. Carol Rittner, John K. Roth, and Wendy Whitworth (St. Paul, MN: Paragon House, 2004), 259–66.

20. Margaret Brearley, "The Rwandan Genocide and the British Religious Press—Roman Catholic, Anglican and Baptist," in *Genocide in Rwanda,* eds. Carol Rittner, John K. Roth, and Wendy Witworth (St. Paul, MN: Paragon House, 2004), 169–179.

21. Timothy C. Morgan, "Healing Genocide: Ten Years after the Slaughter, Rwandans Begin to Mend Their Torn Nation with a Justice that Is Both Biblical and African," *Christianity Today,* April 2004, 76–83

22. Rainer Klusener, "Islam in Rwanda," Muslim World Initiative, United States Institute of Peace, 2005, http://www.usip.org/muslimworld/bulletin/2005/may.html#feature2.

23. Muslims claim that, unlike the Christian groups, Muslims in Rwanda protected the Tutsi victims and prevented them from being killed. Because there were moderate Hutu and Christians, however, it would be misleading to say that Christians did not protect the victims of the genocide.

24. Laurie Goering, "Islam Blooms in Rwanda Genocide's Wake," Chicago Tribune Online, August 5, 2002, http://www.zawaj.com/editorials/rwanda_islam.html.

25. M. D. Abdullah, "Growth of the Muslim Community in Rwanda," Muslimedia, December 16–31, 2002, http://www.muslimedia.com/archives/special02/rwan-muslims.htm.

26. Rwandan Constitution, Title 1: Articles 7, 16, and 18.

27. Scott R. Feil, *Preventing Genocide: How the Early Use of Force Might Have Succeeded in Rwanda* (New York: Carnegie Corporation, April 1998), 35.

3

Literature and Media

The story is our escort; without it, we are blind. Does the blind man own his escort? No, neither do we the story; rather it is the story that owns us and directs us.

—Chinua Achebe, 1987

An intricate relationship exists between memory and history, with African literature demonstrating that the brain is mightier than the pen. Memory is a powerful means of preserving the past from being forgotten, from fading, and from extinction. With a dearth of written documents, the centrality of oral literature cannot be ignored in reconstructing the history of Rwanda and in unearthing the rich culture and customs of the society. As a preliterate society, Rwanda belongs to the group of African peoples whose languages were not committed to writing until the coming of the Europeans. This prompted the Rwandan peoples to develop a culture of recollecting their history, traditions, experiences, and laws by memory. Rwanda possesses a considerable body of oral literature, which constitutes a strong part of its cultural history. Because Rwandans had no alphabet and no written language, the rich history, culture, and customs have been preserved in oral traditions, both royal and commoner.

Rwandan traditions are well represented in chants, names, myths, poems, proverbs, and songs. The occupational and economic life of the people also is recorded in oral traditions. A large portion of the oral literature has been flavored with mythology, which relates to the beginnings of royalty and centralized political systems. This means that an extensive part of the traditions or oral literature pertains to the Tutsi ruling class. Professional singers in the courts of the rulers performed the function of reciting the royal genealogical list and long verses of praises to the king. The skill is hereditary and is passed from generation to generation. Like palace historians in other parts of Africa, professional singers in Rwanda often recite royal genealogies as well as significant and historical events. Thus, they preserve and from time to time reenact the history, culture, and customs of the Rwandan society.

Written literature did not emerge until late nineteenth century when the Europeans arrived, especially the Roman Catholic priests who introduced Christianity and Western education. Their primary objective was to propagate Christianity, but in the process, they began to introduce European culture and education. This was part of the so-called civilizing mission of the Europeans in the period of imperialism at the end of the nineteenth century. Through biblical education, the missionaries taught Rwandans how to read, write, and commit Bible verses into memory. Gradually, a formal system of education began to replace the traditional, informal mode of instruction. The introduction of Western education, however, did not immediately displace the traditional form of education; instead, they coexisted. Given the fact that early missionaries spoke French and Rwanda was colonized by Belgium (French-speaking), French, rather than Kinyarwanda, became the official language of Rwanda.

Many literary works have been produced in French, including those written by indigenous Rwandans. In the postgenocide period, however, English has gained tremendous ground. It is taught in schools and used in government documents. It is expected that more English literature will be published in Rwanda in the future. At present, more written literature exists in French than in either Kinyarwanda or English, but some French books have been translated into English.[1]

ORAL LITERATURE

Oral literature is the storehouse of African culture, history, and folklore. In nonliterate societies, oral literature provides historical evidence of the rich past of the people, and it is part of their living traditions. On many occasions and for different topics, historians have used oral literature to reconstruct the past of African societies. More often than not, elders and palace historians serve as custodians and repositories of oral literature, which is often narrated in stories or performed during special occasions. The oral literature of Rwanda can be classified into three types: the predynastic stories (often described as fairy tales or legends), the royal or official tradition, and the commoner or popular one. Put together, Rwandan oral literature is rich and reveals the wealth of the people's culture and customs. It has formed a significant part of written literature. Some of the stories, however, relate the unpleasant past experiences of interethnic conflicts.

PREDYNASTIC STORIES

Some of the predynastic stories were myths, some were historical, and others taught moral behavior or character building, which constituted the bedrock of Rwandan culture and customs. Around fires in the evening, adults often narrated funny but educative stories. Also, moonlight storytelling took place. The evening period was appropriate not only for relaxation but also for social interaction. Storytelling during the day was prohibited after one story lasted several days and prevented people from working in the fields. The creator god, Imana, was said to be angry with the people for listening to a story instead of working on their farms. He consequently prohibited daylight storytelling.

One of the advantages of storytelling is that it encourages imaginative thinking and self-expression. It is an educative process in which the young ones are indirectly trained to narrate the stories they heard from several storytellers in their own way without loosing the original content. More importantly, they are trained to draw moral lessons from the stories. Stories teach children lessons of love, cooperation, generosity, and loyalty. Stories are also used to teach the children about their culture and heritage.

ROYAL LITERATURE

Copious information exists on the royal literature of the Rwandan society because past history focused mainly on the chronology of events during the reigns of kings. Royal literature consisted of fixed traditions, which were created, memorized, and preserved by specific families of professional singers and regulated by the Tutsi kings. The royal traditions have been transmitted from generation to generation. Royal court historians and their family members often enjoyed a high level of prestige, given their ability to recite long genealogical list of rulers. Along with sociocultural institutions, royal literature also has existed in Rwanda for centuries. Four of the royal traditions exist: *ubucurabwenge* (a royal genealogical list), often recited at the coronation of a new king by the *abacurabwenge* ("forgers of intelligence," or royal court historians); *ibitekerezo* (a collection of royal myths); *ibisigo* (a collection of royal poetry); and *ubwiru* (a set of royal rituals). *Ubucurabwenge* is considered a wisdom literature, and other traditions were structured around it. The *abacurabwenge* royal court historians were the officials who preserved and recited the *ubucurabwenge,* which is also known as the *Amasekuruza y'Abami* (Genealogy of the Kings). The *ibisigo* represents a collection of symbolic poetry and consists of approximately 176 poems. An early Rwandan poem states, "the Sovereign could never have a rival, he is the One and Only, the Irreproachable," signifying the supremacy of the king over his people.

Two prominent names in Rwandan oral literature were Kigwa and Gihanga. Traditions believe that Kigwa (fallen), a legendary figure, descended from heaven and became the first Tutsi king. To establish his divinely ordained authority to rule and to legitimize his position and power, Kigwa purportedly created the *abiru* (court musicians and ritualists), which became one of the most important religious and political institutions in Rwanda.[2] The establishment of the *abiru* suggests the complexity and intricacy of the interactions between religion and politics in the early history of Rwanda. One of Kigwa's successors was Gihanga (creator) who became the cultural hero of the Rwandan people and who founded the first empire.[3] Gihanga has been portrayed as being skilled in many things: politics, religion, and technology. In central Rwanda, Gihanga not only was celebrated as a dynastic founder, but the cult of Gihanga also was created to attach religious and political importance to his name. Jan Vansina argues that because traditions surrounding Kigwa and Gihanga were legends with no direct historical foundation, their authenticity is questionable.[4] These names, however, continue to be mentioned in the royal oral literature of Rwanda. As part of the royal oral literature, the *intore* dancers from time to time reenact the warrior tradition of the Tutsi, and the *tambourinaires* (drummers) play a major role in preserving Rwandan culture and traditions.

Although it is possible to penetrate the past of Rwanda through these traditions, they offer some problems. One of the problems is that events are not often narrated in chronological sequence, presumably because the human brain is prone to lapses. Another is the possibility of deliberate distortion, but to guard against that, there are sanctions. Another major problem is the lack of dates. Eclipses of the sun were used to date events. Archaeologists are able to analyze and date artifacts recovered from the ground.

LITERATURE IN KINYARWANDA

Although Kinyarwanda is widely spoken and has been adopted as the language of instruction at the elementary-school level, very little written literature exists in the language. That is not surprising because Rwandan literature has been essentially oral. The absence of a writing culture and the prevalence of oral literature were the primary reasons for Rwandans not producing literature in Kinyarwanda. Rwandans do have a general awareness about the importance of promoting literature in Kinyarwanda, especially for the young people who should be taught to be proud of the culture and language. Children's books are now being published or translated from French or English into Kinyarwanda. Children's literature in Kinyarwanda is promoted in order for young people to be aware of and proud of their cultural and historical background. Many also believe that literature in Kinyarwanda can help in the rebuilding of the country. Listening to stories, reading, and writing in Kinyarwanda has provided a foundation and motivation for children to read and write in either French or English. The culture of reading must begin with Kinyarwanda. That is why Editions Bakame (founded in 1995) began as a publishing house with the following objectives:

1. Creating and promoting youth literature based on Rwandan culture.
2. Instilling a reading culture in children.
3. Forming partnerships with associations having the same objectives.[5]

Novelists such as J. Mukarugira have published in Kinyarwanda, but their works are not well known.

Christian missionaries who learned to speak and read Kinyarwanda translated the Bible, prayer books, hymn books, the catechism, and other books into Kinyarwanda for the spiritual nourishment of their congregants. For example, Reverend Halord of the Missionary Society began the translation of Christian literature into Kinyarwanda in 1926. The first Kinyarwanda common-language Bible with deuterocanon has just been completed, and there is the possibility of reprinting and distributing the Kinyarwanda Roman Catholic Bible.

POETRY IN KINYARWANDA

Poetry was a rich and integral part of the Rwandan culture and history. The *abasizi* (poets) often recounted poetry in a complex manner and in the Kinyarwanda language, capturing and extolling the accomplishments of the rulers in genealogical sequence. Rwandan poetry is symbolic and interwoven with religious beliefs. For example, the saying *Umwami si umuntu ni imaana* (The king is not a man, he is a god) demonstrates that even though the king is human, he is a god. This shows the semidivine nature and power of the king. Royal poetry not only referred to the sacredness of Rwandan kingship, but it also served as the core of Rwandan history. Rwandan tradition holds that a queen mother who was a poet and in quest of cultural revival established a royal institution known as the Seat of Poets in order to compose, preserve, promote, and train the youth in Rwandan culture, royal history, and poetry.[6]

The Tutsi were particularly recognized for their poetry, designed to legitimize and memorialize their political power and status. Such political or dynastic poems were generally called *ibisigo;* that is, what has been bequeathed to prosperity. The poems chronicled the origins, warrior traditions, and political prowess of the Tutsi ruling class. As Liz Gunner rightly put it, "Poetry was, in a way, the heartbeat of royalty."[7] The Tutsi had reason to preserve their royalty in poems because they struggled against hostile neighbors and European imperialism. Western influence as a result of colonialism brought about a shift in Rwandan poetry from prodynastic to antidynastic themes.[8]

Alexis Kagame was the pioneer of written poetry in Rwanda. He collected 176 poems, which he published in his *La Poésie dynastique au Rwanda* (Dynastic Poetry of Rwanda), published in 1951. His poems were historical, political, social, and religious and based on oral literature and mythology. His first historical poem was *Matabaro Ajya Iburayi* (Matabaro Leaves for Europe), written between 1938 and 1939. Between 1947 and 1951, Kagame published a three-volume series called *Isoko y'Amajyambere* (Sources of Progress). His religious poem "The Singer of the Lord of Creation" was a masterpiece. Jean-Baptiste Mutabaruka, C. Rugamba, A. Gapira, and F. X. Munyarugerero are some leading Rwandan poets in the postindependence period. Most of the poems have been written in verse form.

DRAMA

Drama, which is the act of putting ideas into words and actions, is cultural, but it was an unpopular aspect of the social life of the Rwandan people in the precolonial times. Other kinds of performances existed, but no reference is made to drama in the oral literature of Rwanda. The common people in the rural areas, whose primary preoccupation was farming, were illiterate. Rwandans, especially the royalty, enjoyed some entertainment in their palaces.

Stage drama in Rwanda was a product of European influence. It began with French teachers who trained their pupils to perform plays written in the French language. As Rwandan teachers emerged, they began to write and perform plays in Kinyarwanda. Writing drama requires experience and knowledge of the cultural, social, and political background, and that is why the early form of drama in Rwanda focused on political aspects. Some plays have been written in Kinyarwanda, others have been written in French and English for those living in the urban centers. In schools and universities, drama is becoming popular. Most of the plays focused on the social aspects of Rwandan culture and customs, including dowry, illiteracy, arranged marriages,

erbs are used to appreciate, to warn, to reveal the wealth identity and
th of a society's culture, and to teach historical and moral lessons. For
ple, the Rwandan proverb *Abantu ntibava inda imwe bava inkono imwe*
fraternity is not about blood, it is about sharing) refers to the blood
onship that was geared toward sharing of love with one another. A witty
g states, "In a court of fowls, the cockroach never wins his case," indicat-
hat poor persons do not receive justice because of their weak and
uential condition. Having faced numerous tragedies in history and in pur-
f peace, Rwandans say in proverb, *Ukize inkuba arayiganira* (If you
ed a tragedy you should speak about it). Another Rwandan proverb
Uburere buruta ubuvuke (Upbringing is more important than birth).
hough Rwandans believe that tragedies are part of life, talking about
s a fundamental part of the healing process. To emphasize cooperation
orking together as a team, a proverb states, "People helping one another
ing an elephant into the house." Rwandans warn about the danger of
words in the proverb, "If your mouth turns into a knife, it will cut off
ps." Proverbs promoting peace and unity feature in artworks such as
. One such proverb states, *Agasozi kagufi kagushyikiriza akarekare*
ing even a short hill will bring us to a higher point).[12]

EN LITERATURE

first European entered Rwanda in 1891, and when European mission-
ived, they began to record Rwandan history with dates. Following the
aries were Belgian anthropologists and historians who collected oral
ns to write the history of Rwanda. Similarly, Africans such as Jan
have used oral traditions to reconstruct the history of Rwanda. Most
early books have focused on the history of Rwanda but did not
ze the culture and customs of the Rwandan people. In the wake of
genocide, written literature has concentrated on ethnic conflicts,
ultural relations. Much of the written literature is now published in
nch and English.

any indigenous people were able to produce written works primarily
f a very limited access to Western education. Alexis Kagame, a Tutsi
Catholic priest, historian, ethnologist, poet, and philosopher, has
many written works on Rwanda, including poems in French and
nda. Born into the family of court historians, Kagame used his vast
e of the royal literature to unfold the past history of Rwanda.
ly directing his writings to the Rwandan audience, Kagame col-
me oral sources and transposed them into written form. This
him to write in the national language, and translations into French

alcoholism, drugs, juvenile delinquency, and prostitut
conflict between traditional and modern culture. Tl
these radio dramas and specifies what playwrights ca
to Jean-Marie V. Rurangwa, few playwrights in Rwa
international languages because the Belgian coloni
sequent administrations did not support and prom
counts for why for many years there was no nati
theater troupe, and no publishing houses for liter;
drama writing has therefore not been lucrative in R

Since the end of the genocide, the National Uni
Center for Art has been promoting drama and w
reach the common people with positive ideas an
drama also helps rebuild and strengthen ethnic r
mental organizations provide funding for series of
equality, tolerance, and unity. Emerging playwrigh
mana, E. Gasana, and P. Mukahigiro, who are e
drama by focusing on cultural and social aspects

LITERATURE IN FOREIGN LANGUAGES

In the postindependence period, foreign w
Rwandans have written primarily in the French l;
(1912–1981) was one of the foremost indige
books, poems, and articles in French. Yollan
writer who survived the genocide and now liv
books, *La mort ne veut pas de moi* (Death Does
pas peur de savoir (Don't Be Afraid to Know, 1

As mentioned previously, literature in Engli
because French was the dominant language; h
produced in English. A U.S.-born author, Ver
the Glutton: A Bantu Tale from Rwanda (1993
also have been published. Since the genocide
lished, and many of them make vague referer
ture of Rwanda.[11] Because the government
English language, it will be possible for more i
original works in English.

PROVERBS AS ORAL LITERATURE

Proverbs and witty sayings *(imigani)* con
ety's culture. They are used on various oc

alcoholism, drugs, juvenile delinquency, and prostitution. They also emphasize conflict between traditional and modern culture. The government regulates these radio dramas and specifies what playwrights can write about. According to Jean-Marie V. Rurangwa, few playwrights in Rwanda write in national and international languages because the Belgian colonial government and subsequent administrations did not support and promote playwriting. This accounts for why for many years there was no national theater, no national theater troupe, and no publishing houses for literary writings.[9] Drama and drama writing has therefore not been lucrative in Rwanda.

Since the end of the genocide, the National University of Rwanda (NUR) Center for Art has been promoting drama and writing of plays in order to reach the common people with positive ideas and to educate them. Radio drama also helps rebuild and strengthen ethnic relations. Some nongovernmental organizations provide funding for series of radio dramas that focus on equality, tolerance, and unity. Emerging playwrights include F. Byuma, Nsabimana, E. Gasana, and P. Mukahigiro, who are educating the youth through drama by focusing on cultural and social aspects of the Rwandan society.

LITERATURE IN FOREIGN LANGUAGES

In the postindependence period, foreign writers as well as indigenous Rwandans have written primarily in the French language. Abbe Alexis Kagame (1912–1981) was one of the foremost indigenous writers who published books, poems, and articles in French. Yollande Mukagasana, a Rwandan writer who survived the genocide and now lives in Europe, has written two books, *La mort ne veut pas de moi* (Death Doesn't Want Me, 1997) and *N'aie pas peur de savoir* (Don't Be Afraid to Know, 1999), about her experiences.

As mentioned previously, literature in English was uncommon in Rwanda because French was the dominant language; however, some works have been produced in English. A U.S.-born author, Verna Aardema, wrote *Sebugugugu the Glutton: A Bantu Tale from Rwanda* (1993).[10] Numerous academic books also have been published. Since the genocide, several books have been published, and many of them make vague reference to the early history and culture of Rwanda.[11] Because the government of Rwanda is promoting the English language, it will be possible for more indigenous Rwandans to publish original works in English.

PROVERBS AS ORAL LITERATURE

Proverbs and witty sayings *(imigani)* constitute an integral part of a society's culture. They are used on various occasions and for different reasons.

Proverbs are used to appreciate, to warn, to reveal the wealth identity and wealth of a society's culture, and to teach historical and moral lessons. For example, the Rwandan proverb *Abantu ntibava inda imwe bava inkono imwe* (Real fraternity is not about blood, it is about sharing) refers to the blood relationship that was geared toward sharing of love with one another. A witty saying states, "In a court of fowls, the cockroach never wins his case," indicating that poor persons do not receive justice because of their weak and uninfluential condition. Having faced numerous tragedies in history and in pursuit of peace, Rwandans say in proverb, *Ukize inkuba arayiganira* (If you survived a tragedy you should speak about it). Another Rwandan proverb states *Uburere buruta ubuvuke* (Upbringing is more important than birth).

Although Rwandans believe that tragedies are part of life, talking about them is a fundamental part of the healing process. To emphasize cooperation and working together as a team, a proverb states, "People helping one another can bring an elephant into the house." Rwandans warn about the danger of spoken words in the proverb, "If your mouth turns into a knife, it will cut off your lips." Proverbs promoting peace and unity feature in artworks such as baskets. One such proverb states, *Agasozi kagufi kagushyikiriza akarekare* (Climbing even a short hill will bring us to a higher point).[12]

Written Literature

The first European entered Rwanda in 1891, and when European missionaries arrived, they began to record Rwandan history with dates. Following the missionaries were Belgian anthropologists and historians who collected oral traditions to write the history of Rwanda. Similarly, Africans such as Jan Vansina have used oral traditions to reconstruct the history of Rwanda. Most of these early books have focused on the history of Rwanda but did not emphasize the culture and customs of the Rwandan people. In the wake of the 1994 genocide, written literature has concentrated on ethnic conflicts, not on cultural relations. Much of the written literature is now published in both French and English.

Not many indigenous people were able to produce written works primarily because of a very limited access to Western education. Alexis Kagame, a Tutsi Roman Catholic priest, historian, ethnologist, poet, and philosopher, has produced many written works on Rwanda, including poems in French and Kinyarwanda. Born into the family of court historians, Kagame used his vast knowledge of the royal literature to unfold the past history of Rwanda. Specifically directing his writings to the Rwandan audience, Kagame collected some oral sources and transposed them into written form. This prompted him to write in the national language, and translations into French were intended to let the outside world know the rich history and culture of Rwanda. He collected "stories from bards, traditional poets and storytellers of Rwandan oral tradition passed through some transformations and linguistic adaptations of the initial esoteric language."[13] One of his earliest poems was *Indyohesha-Birayi* (The Flavor-Enhancer of Potatoes), which was a humorous and satiric poem about a royal banquet.[14] Alexis Kagame published the *Inganji Karinga* (The Victorious Drums) in 1943. The book embodies the mind and wisdom of Rwandan literature and contains the genealogical list of the Rwandan kings and the military prowess and success of the Tutsi rulers and prescribes ritual observances. The palace historians who preserve the genealogical list are referred to as the *abacurabwenge* (forgers of intelligence or genealogists) because their responsibility of recounting the regnal list involves wisdom and ability to remember names and events.

As a Christian and a defender of Tutsi political traditions, Kagame wrote the *Le code des institutions politiques au Rwanda* in 1952 in defense of the old social order as reformed along Christian lines. Another Rwandan author was J. Saverio Naigiziki (1915–1984), whose novel *Escapade Rwandaise* (Rwandan Adventure), an autobiography written in French, was published in 1950. In 1954, Naigiziki published a novel *L'Optimiste* (The Optimist), which was about the marriage between a Hutu man and a Tutsi woman. As the colonial language and the one used and taught in schools, it was not surprising that French became the main literary language in Rwanda. Like Kagame, Naigiziki also wrote on religion and culture, focusing on conflict between cultural tradition and modernity.

MEDIA

The media have a means of disseminating useful information to the people. It plays a major role in the sociopolitical life of the society. The traditional way of circulating news was through palace officials. In the colonial period, the Belgians controlled the media. By 1991, only Radio Rwanda, owned by the government, existed. As the mouthpiece of the government, the Radio Rwanda announced primarily political matters and speeches of Juvénal Habyarimana, the president. The radio station did not have any significant impact on the life of the people in the rural areas because not many people owned radio sets; in the urban centers such as Butare and Kigali, however, many households possessed radios.[15] The lack of radios may be attributed to the high rate of illiteracy and poverty, which was a result of the generally poor economy. Those who did not have radios listened to news in bars.

To present the voice of the Tutsi to the public, the Rwandan Patriotic Front (RPF) founded its own radio station (Radio Muhabura), but it had a limited

signal and a limited audience. Although it was antigovernment, the radio station tried to promote the coexistence of the people of Rwanda. In August
1993, the Radio (Radio et Television Libres des Mille Collines, RTLM) was
established by Hutu hard-liners as a private radio station, but its programs
and broadcasts were progovernment. It broadcast in French, Kinyarwanda,
and Swahili. Radio Rwanda (the national radio station) and RTLM ran similar programs and news items, but RTLM became more popular for its lively
music. RTLM operated as an interactive radio station by sometimes inviting
people to express their opinion in public. The radio station soon became the
voice of extremism because during the genocide it called for a total war in
order to "exterminate the cockroaches," the Tutsi. Instead of news, the radio
was disseminating propaganda, delivering the message of hate, and broadcasting the names of people to be killed.[16] Anti-Tutsi music dominated the radio.
According to Nik Gowing, "In Rwanda, hate radio—Radio Mille Collines—
systematically laid the groundwork for mass slaughter from the moment it
was licensed in July 1993."[17]

Following the conclusion of the genocide in 1994, the British government's
Overseas Development Administration, the United Nations High Commissioner for Refugees, and a consortium of British nongovernmental organizations established the Great Lakes service, broadcasting in Kinyarwanda and
Kirundi. It was broadcast to the refugees and returnees, providing regional
news items and information on agriculture, health, and reconstruction.
Similarly, Voice of America (VOA) began to broadcast in Kinyarwanda and
Kurundi in July 1996. These radio stations and programs were intended to
provide unbiased information not only for people in Rwanda but also for
people in Burundi and elsewhere in Central Africa.

NEWSPAPERS

Like the radio, few newspapers and magazines existed in Rwanda after the
colonial period. Published in either French or Kinyarwanda, the newspapers
carried little international news and were read mainly in the urban areas. The
newspapers and periodicals had a limited circulation as a result of lack of
education and poverty. The sale of the newspapers was low because Rwandans
developed the culture of group reading. Newspapers in circulation after independence included the *Rwanda Carrefour d'Afrique* (Crossroads of Africa), a
French monthly publication that provided information on Rwanda and
government activities because it was published in Kigali by the Ministry of
Information and Tourism.

One of the earliest independent monthly newspapers in Rwanda was
Kinyamateka, published in the Kinyarwanda language. Founded in 1933 and

Imvaho Nshya, a Rwandan newspaper in Kinyarwanda. Courtesy of the author.

affiliated with the Roman Catholic Church, *Kinyamateka* provided primarily religious news. It increased its circulation in 1955 and became a vehicle through which political ideas of the Hutu government were disseminated. Its readers were mostly members of the church. The bimonthly *Dialogue,* another independent paper founded in 1967 by the Roman Catholic Church, also enjoyed protection from the government. Although these two papers remained strongly associated with the government, their influence and power to criticize the government, especially on the treatment of the Tutsi, was significantly restrained in the postindependence period. Because of the political restructuring that was taking place, *Kinyamateka* ceased to be a mouthpiece of the government and became an independent paper in 1988.

The founding of the Kinyarwanda-language *Kanguka* (Wake Up) in 1988 marked the beginning of an independent press in Rwanda. Because its founder was a Tutsi businessman, the Hutu-controlled government established *Kangura* (Wake Them Up) as a state-owned newspaper in October 1990. *Kangura* was published essentially in Kinyarwanda, but with some articles in French. It has been operating as a medium of hate media, publicly denouncing and demonizing Tutsis and the RPF. In December 1990, *Kangura* published the "Hutu Ten Commandments" that called for Hutu power in

Rwanda. Published twice a month, *Kangura* became an extremist magazine, writing pungent anti-Tutsi articles and using political cartoons and caricatures to demonstrate ethnic difference and to send messages of hate to the readers. Names and addresses of intended victims were published in the magazine shortly before the genocide. *Kangura* stopped publishing in April 1994. Other newspapers that were founded in 1990 included *Umuranga, Ijambo, Isibo,* and *Le democrate.* Objective news or reports were difficult to obtain because the newspapers were either ethnically or politically biased. In addition, the government's close watch on the media and the arbitrary arrests and detention of journalists restricted what journalists could publish. By 1992, as many as thirty newspapers were published in Rwanda.

The role of the newspapers in the genocide cannot be overstressed. Ethnically defined newspapers were established: the Tutsi *Kanguka* and the Hutu *Kangura.* The *Kangura* had the upper hand, being government controlled. In the trials of those involved in the genocide, some newspaper officials were found guilty. In the judgment, the judges argued, "The power of the media to create and destroy human values comes with great responsibility. Those who control the media are accountable for its consequences."[18]

PERIODICALS

During the postgenocide period, only 28 newspapers, periodicals, and monthlies exist in Rwanda and none are published on daily basis. Due to the irregular production, the periodicals sometimes carry late news. This situation has slightly changed because the number of newspapers and periodicals is growing. *Rwanda Carrefour d'Afrique* (Crossroads of Africa), *Kinyamateka, The New Times,* and *Imvaho Nshya* are periodicals that carry information on national, African, and world events and religious, social, and cultural news. Only one television station (TV Rwanda) and six radio stations are in operation.

For a long time, foreign writers have dominated Rwandan media, but to reverse this trend, the School of Journalism and Communication was established at the National University of Rwanda in 1996. Whether foreign or indigenous, journalists in Rwanda face the enormous challenge of publishing unbiased news and articles that are geared toward rebuilding the country by promoting peace and unity.

Oral literature flourished in Rwanda before and during the dynastic period, and the traditions have passed from one generation to the next. Although kingship has been abolished, the traditions that surrounded its establishment, the names and accomplishments of the rulers, are still remembered in oral traditions. Historians, anthropologists, sociologists, and ethnologists have garnered useful information for the reconstruction of Rwanda's past.

Oral literature is a valuable source of history and its custodians are both informants and historians, but the spread of Western education has made written literature more widely circulated than oral traditions. Oral literature still exists and storytelling is practiced, and because of their invaluable contributions to the historical past of Rwanda, storytellers are still admired and well respected in the society. They assist researchers in remembering and reconstructing the past. Folktales, myths, poems, proverbs, and stories that teach cultural, historical, and moral lessons now appear in written literature. Through these, the youth are informed of the historical and rich past as well as the wealth of their culture and customs. Butare has become the intellectual center of Rwanda where a literary scene has been created and the cultural past of the country preserved in the National Museum of Rwanda. A section of the museum has been designated to prehistory and the dynastic period of Rwandan history. A chronological list of rulers, based on oral traditions and written documents, is displayed in the museum. Apparently, the National Museum has become a viable research center.

Since the genocide, written literature on Rwanda has significantly increased. Many of the works make vague reference to the past but concentrate on the events of the genocide. Alongside the written literature are oral eyewitness and victim accounts of their ordeals. The complicity of the media is not in doubt. The media became instruments used to encourage hate and violence and to promote propaganda and disunity during the genocide. The media were used to promote the social revolutions that have taken place in Rwandan history. History has recorded not only the dark moments of Rwanda but also the role of the media in encouraging violence. The media in the postgenocide period is turning things around by publishing positive news and promoting integration.

In the past, the media played a destructive and ethnically divisive role, but now, it can become an agent of reconstruction, a medium of positive expression, and an instrument of rebuilding the devastated country. The media should shift from hate to peace, and the government should remove stringent limitations on the media and allow freedom of speech. Newspapers, magazines, and radio should report the truth and promote national integration and peace. Ethnic affiliation is no longer emphasized in papers, and constructive articles that voice the opinion of the people on hope and a better future are published. In an article published in *The New Times,* the author indicated that "The unity of Rwandans which has to be realized in practical terms is a crucial facet in a totality of factors that now give hope that tomorrow will be better and sustainable. It is not a question of rhetoric or propaganda."[19]

The improvement on the level of literacy will enable more Rwandans to read newspapers and magazines and become more politically conscious. The government holds the pertinent task of promoting education at all levels in order for the people outside the major cities who speak primarily Kinyarwanda to have access to French and English newspapers and magazines.

Some Works by Alexis Kagame

Matabaro Ajya Iburayi (Matabaro Leaves for Europe) (1938–1939).

Inganji Karinga (The Victorious Drums), vol. 1 (Kabgayi, Rwanda: Editions Royales, 1943).

Inganji Karinga (The Victorious Drums), vol. 2 (Kabgayi, Rwanda: Editions Royales, 1947).

Umwaduko w'Abazungu muli Afrika yo hagati (The Arrival of the Europeans in Central Africa) (Kabgayi, Rwanda: Editions Royales, 1947).

La Poésie dynastique au Rwanda (Dynastic Poetry of Rwanda) (Brussels, Belgium: Académie Royale des Sciences d'Outre-Mer, 1951).

Isoko y'Amäjyambere (Sources of Progress), vols. 1–3 (Kabgayi, Rwanda: Editions Morales, 1949–1951).

Umulirimbyi wa Nyili-ibiremwa (The Singer of the Lord of Creation) (Butare, Rwanda: Astrida, 1950).

Le code des institutions politiques de Rwanda précolonial (Brussels, Belgium: IRCB, 1952).

Les organizations socio-familiales de l'ancien Rwanda (Brussels, Belgium: Académie Royale des Sciences d'Outre-Mer, 1954).

Le pluralisme ethnique et cultural dans de Rwanda-Urundi. Compterendu de la 30e session de l'Indici (Brussels, Belgium: Editions du Marais, 1957).

La Philosophie Bantu-Rwandaise de L'être (Brussels, Belgium: Académie Royale des Sciences Coloniales, 1956).

Introduction aux grands genres lyriques de l'ancien Rwanda (Introduction to the Great Lyrical Poems of Ancient Rwanda) (Butare: Editions Universitaires due Rwanda, 1969).

Un abrégé de l'éthno-histoire du Rwanda précolonial, vol. 1 (Butare: Editions Universitaires de Rwanda, 1972).

Un abrégé de l'éthno-histoire du Rwanda précolonial, vol. 2 (Butare: Editions Universitaires de Rwanda, 1975).

NOTES

1. Jan Vansina's *Le Rwanda ancien: le royaume nyiginya* has been translated into English, as *Antecedents to Modern Rwanda: The Nyiginya Kingdom,* by the author himself.

2. Lucy Mair, *African Societies* (London: Cambridge University Press, 1974), 171.

3. Jan Vansina, *Antecedents to Modern Rwanda: The Nyiginya Kingdom* (Madison: University of Wisconsin Press, 2004), 10.

4. Ibid., 223, note 36.

5. Hellen Mwiholeze, "A Woman Fighting for Children's Literature in Kinyarwanda," *The New Times,* December 1–2, 2004, 9.

6. Rose-Marie Mukarutabana, "Gakondo: The Royal Poetry," n.d., http://webspinners.com/Gakondo/en/Poetry/index.php.

7. Liz Gunner, "Africa and Orality," in *The Cambridge History of African and Caribbean Literature,* ed. Abiola Irele and Simon Gikandi (Cambridge: Cambridge University Press, 2004): 1–10.

8. Ibid., 1–10.

9. Jean-Marie V. Rurangwa, "Writing Drama Today," n.d., http://www.uiowa.edu/~iwp/EVEN/documents/Drama-Rurangwa.pdf.

10. Verna Aardema has published many books based on stories from different parts of Africa.

11. For example, Gerard Prunier, *The Rwanda Crisis: History of a Genocide* (New York: Columbia University Press, 1995); Rosamond Halsey Carr, *Land of a Thousand Hills: My Life in Rwanda* (New York: Viking/Allen Lane, 1999).

12. "The Women of Gitarama—Landing at Macy's against the Odds," http://www.nbpc.tv/mediacenter/africaopen/article-02.php.

13. Anthere Nzabatsinda, "'Traduttore Traditore'? Alexis Kagame's Transposition of Kinyarwanda Poetry into French," *Journal of African Cultural Studies* 12, no. 2 (December 1999): 203–10.

14. Ibid. The poem was first published in 1949 and reprinted in 1977.

15. In rural areas, 27.3 percent of the households had radios by 1991, but in urban centers, 58.7 percent of households owned radios. Northwestern University Library, Evanston, Illinois, *Recensement général de la population et de l'habitat au 15 août 1991* (Kigali, Rwanda: Service National de Recensement, July 1993), 31.

16. Russell Smith, "The Impact of Hate Media in Rwanda," BBC News Online, December 3, 2003, http://news.bbc.co.uk/1/hi/world/africa/3257748.stm.

17. Nik Gowing, *Media Coverage: Help or Hindrance in Conflict Prevention,* (Washington, DC: Carnegie Commission on Preventing Deadly Conflict, 1997), 30.

18. Sharon LaFraniere, "Three Guilty in Rwanda Genocide," *The New York Times,* December 4, 2003, A1.

19. Peter Niyinbizi, "Rwanda Now Is a Land of Hope," *The New Times,* March 8–9, 2006, 9.

4

Art and Architecture/Housing

Art and architecture add aesthetic beauty and flavor to African culture; they are portraits of a rich culture.

—Julius O. Adekunle, 2006

The creation of art was an integral part of human culture from the beginning. The knowledge and expression of art rose out of human ability and ingenuity to not only beautify the environment but also to protect and to make life easier. Archaeological discoveries in Europe and different parts of Africa have indicated the development of art in various forms. The use of bones, stones, metals, sculpture, painting, and drawing provide great insight into how early human beings developed impressive and sophisticated forms of art. Circumstances dictated by religion and occupation sometimes led to the creation of art. The early civilization of Egypt produced outstanding works of art, which other societies in Africa subsequently learned and improved upon. Art is a mark of identity for a society and it is a status symbol. Lynn Mackenzie made the important point that "Art helped organize society and solve its problems" and "when art functioned as sign of social distinction, the display of certain objects could indicate kinship, political rank, or economic success."[1] Many ancient artworks in the form of paintings of images of animals on rock slabs in caves, sculptures of clay heads, and human figures have been found in several locations in Africa.

The richness of Rwandan culture is demonstrated in the variety of artwork, with most of them satisfying everyday needs, such as ornaments, baskets, and pots. Ceramic, pottery, basketry, wood carving, and metalwork are mostly made in the rural areas but sold primarily at the Centre for the Formation of Arts in Kigali. Skilled artisans created and designed the artworks that carry symbolic meanings and that serve religious purposes. Art as well as other aspects of traditional and cultural life of Rwanda are in some cases unique and sometimes similar to those found in other parts of Africa. Tutsi rulers wore ornaments made by Rwandan artisans.

ART

From ancient times to the contemporary period, examples of art include wood carving (such as images, doors, and musical instruments), house posts, drawings, masks, utensils, tools, and weapons. Rock paintings (drawings and paintings on cave walls), engraving on pottery, decorations, and inscriptions on baskets constitute an important part of art. One of the advantages of art is that it illuminates the understanding of African traditions. Artists were specialists who developed and transmitted the skill within the family from one generation to the next. Their works were predominantly traditional, and art objects were used in religious rituals, in initiation ceremonies, and for economic purposes. Some objects of African art reflect the socioeconomic status of an individual, a family, or a community. They also may be symbols of position and power, such as kings' crowns, headgear, and the staff of authority.

Rwandan wood carving showing household materials. Courtesy of Dr. Eleazar Ziherambere.

Rwandan artistic expressions have been demonstrated in pottery, basketry, and music. They also have been expressed in the clothing, ritual materials, weapons, and poetic genres of the royal courts. In the Nyiginya Kingdom in central Rwanda, artists and artisans often worked in the palace.[2]

TRADITIONAL ART

In Rwandan traditional art, men controlled carving (in wood, stones, and metals) and sculpture, whereas women dominated the ceramic and basket industries. A carver has an idea of the artistic work he intends to produce when he begins to work on block of wood with a sharp knife. According to Glenn King, "a skilled practitioner … has a clear vision of his final product without recourse to any model or sketch."[3] Drums, bowls, and jugs are some products of wood carving. Different colors and patterns of linear decorations make traditional art very beautiful.

Through basket making, wood carving, pottery, sculpture, and house decorations, Rwandans beautifully express their ingenuity in traditional art. House decoration was the exclusive artwork of women. The walls and floors were often decorated with cow-dung paintings, with black, brown, and white whorls and other geometric patterns.[4] Paintings, wood carvings, and baskets are reflected in house decorations.

TEXTILES AND FASHION

The clothing in Rwanda has undergone a series of changes, even though Rwandans have always worn light and colorful clothing because of the year-round warm weather. Many centuries ago, animal skins constituted the clothing of the people. In many parts of precolonial tropical Africa, bark cloth was very common as a fabric. Not surprisingly, in Rwanda, Hutu men wore goat skins and bark shirts, and the Twa wore skins from antelopes, sheep or goats. The aristocratic and wealthy Tutsi wore cow, leopard, or lion skins. Hutu girls wore belts of either lion or leopard skin. As a mark of wealth, importance, and ethnic distinction, Tutsi girls wore belts of lion or leopard skin with fringes. Women adorned themselves with headbands, bracelets, ornamental jewelry, and rings. Rwandans are proud of their traditional dress.

Clothing witnessed a change in the wake of Rwandan commercial relations with the Arab and Persian merchants in the Swahili states along the coast of East Africa. Although Rwandan women were engaged in producing hand-loomed clothes, colorful, beautiful, and light clothes were imported from the coast.

In the aftermath of colonization and modernization, Western influence has impacted the mode of dressing. After gaining independence, successive

Rwandan governments encouraged the wearing of Western-style clothes. Traces of the traditional mode of dressing still exist in the rural areas, but Western clothes predominate in cities. Imported clothes, such as T-shirts and suits, from the Western world and neighboring African countries are sold in Butare, Kigali, and other cities. Most of the fabrics worn by women are manufactured in the Netherlands. A textile industry, established in Kigali, has been producing tons of various kinds of fabrics on an annual basis. Rwandan tailors make different styles of pants, shorts, and shirts. A recent survey on fashion shows the continuing popularity of Western-style clothes in Rwanda. According to the survey, 25 percent of the people wear traditional clothes, whereas 38 percent preferred Western-style clothes.[5]

SCULPTURE

African sculpture has a long history, dating back to the Stone Age. During the Iron Age, African sculpture became more sophisticated and more naturalistic. Although decorations, shapes, and styles differed from one society to the next and new techniques were adopted from time to time, there is evidence of continuity with the society's traditions. As in other parts of Africa, Rwandan traditional sculpture depicted rulers and ancestral heroes, indicating the cultural, political, and religious influence on sculpture. Sculptural works were often showcased in the king's palace, public places, or religious shrines.

African sculpture been described as frontal, meaning the figures face forward. Wooden sculptures show prisoners transporting a white man in a hammock, and each sculptor integrates his central motif to the artwork. Sculptures, made by Rwandans in the Democratic Republic of the Congo and Uganda, are brought to Butare and Kigali for sale. Bronze sculpture depicting tradition, power, and wealth in the form of masks and figures are commonplace in Rwanda. The sculptures were made for religious and secular purposes. Because Rwanda had economic contacts with the Swahili states, Arab sculptures were introduced.

Sculpture may be traditional, contemporary, or abstract. Political occurrences in Rwanda have provided new grounds for contemporary artists and sculptors to create works of art on the genocide. Sculpture may be life-size or monumental. For example, a magnificent 30-foot statue by Epaphrodite Binamungu, a Rwandan indigene, stands in the Butare Memorial Center.[6] Artists from Africa or other parts of the world produce contemporary artworks that relate to the genocide. These artworks have become an important and lasting part of Rwanda's historical past.

PAINTING

Painting is a creative and aesthetic way of displaying a culture. A spectacular aspect of traditional Rwandan art is the cow-dung painting. Houses were decorated with cow dung in different shapes, designs, and colors. Black, brown, and white whorls as well as geometric patterns make the paintings unique and attractive. Houses of wealthy people were particularly well decorated with cow-dung paintings. Painters in Nyakarimbi near the Rusumo Falls cooperate to work together in workshops. In spite of the changes that have taken place, traditional painting continues to meet the political, religious, and social needs of the people. Rwandan artists have not rejected the traditional painting methods and values in favor of abstract art. Instead, they use the traditional background to produce paintings to record historic events.

Mary Cassatt, a U.S. impressionist painter who lived and worked in France, made a painting in about 1891 entitled "The Bath," and it appeared on a Rwandan stamp in 1975.[7] Many aspects of Rwandan culture have been represented on Rwandan postage stamps. Contemporary artists have produced oil paintings that depict the living beauty of Rwanda and the experience of the genocide. At the same time, changes have taken place in the wake of demand and influence of foreigners and tourists.

WOOD CARVING

Wood carving involves a long, complex process and requires specific professional skills. Some of the tools required included an axe, adze, billhook, a grass knife with a long handle, a chisel, angular chisel, a small scraper, and wood of various sizes and length. Among the final products were arrow shafts, awls for piecing, support pillars for huts and for roofs, beehives, canoes, drums, handles for knives and machetes, sheaths for swords, and shields. Figures of animals such as gorillas, flags, and maps have been crafted from wood. Well-decorated wood bottles (gourd containers) and religious images have been carved out of jacaranda and *umusave* wood.

Wood carving depends largely on trees, but because of the continuous damage to the environment through deforestation, the profession is facing some difficulties. Another problem is that wood carving did not bring in substantial income for carvers. As more tourists visit Rwanda and buy carvings, there will be an increased awareness of the beauty and durability as well as the cultural and historical values of the wood carving. Butare, Kigali, and Viaki are the most prominent centers for wood carving. It is customary for Rwandans to share their cultural artifacts in the form of gifts to their

Wood carving of a Rwandan woman
pounding with a mortar and pestle
and carrying her child on her back.
Courtesy of Dr. Eleazar Ziherambere.

friends outside Rwanda. These wood-carved souvenirs come in different
shapes, sizes, and are all representations of the Rwandan cultural heritage.

BASKETRY

Basketry was an integral part of the cultures of preindustrial societies. In
the various centers of ancient civilizations in Africa, basket and mat making
was an important industry. The raw materials such as sisal from the agave
plant, bark, grass, raffia from palm fibers, and reeds were readily available
because they grew everywhere. It is uncertain when Rwandan women first
acquired the knowledge of basketry techniques. In several parts of Africa,
weaving, coiling, and knotting (or looping) techniques were used in the basket industry.

Basket weaving has been a traditional and widespread form of art in
Rwanda, especially by the Tutsi aristocratic women, who specialized in making
small, lidded *agaseke* (small basket). They use a coiling method that has

endured for thousands of years. Although the social status of a basket maker could be identified by the skillful, expressive, and colorful methods used, Tutsi women had sufficient time to master and perfect their skills in basket weaving due to their privileged position. Nature served as an important source for the patterns and colors used in the baskets.

The basket industry contributed substantially to the economic and cultural life of the Rwandan women and their counterparts in Burundi. Made of natural fiber, baskets serve a utilitarian function as well as a mode of aesthetic expression both in the traditional and contemporary setting. Exquisite lidded baskets with beautiful and bright colors and graphic patterns are being produced by women artists. Each of the traditional forms of decoration had a specific name. The main raw materials for basket making include bamboo strips, cypress, and *Eleusine indica,* a type of grass. Banana leaves mixed with raffia stems were used for bags and cushions. The process of production is described as follows:

> The surface of this basket features three rows of a repeating triangular-shaped motif in black. The flat cover of the basket is formed from a coiled cylinder. It is decorated with a black dot at the center, out of which radiate concentric circles in alternating colors—black and natural buff. Surrounding the concentric circles is the same repeated triangular motif seen on the side of the basket. The bottom of the basket features a similar starburstlike motif, but consisting of only a central black dot with a number of radiating black triangles.[8]

Not all baskets have lids, but the conical lids are also intricately woven and have harmonious zigzag ornamentation.[9] Although the finished product is beautiful, the process of weaving is cumbersome, intricate, and painstaking, requiring full concentration and precision. Given the slow process, it has not been possible to produce fine baskets on a large scale. The series of political and social revolutions that Rwanda has gone through have significantly and adversely affected basket production. Tutsi women no longer enjoy their erstwhile privileged position, and today, weaving baskets in the traditional way is done only by older women.

In the traditional setting, baskets were used for various purposes. First lidded baskets *(inkangara)* served as storage containers for personal materials such as clothing, ornaments, headdresses, and shields. Some are used as suitcases. A beautifully made *inkangara* is often given as a special gift to a married woman who is in seclusion. (A period of seclusion is an important part of the Rwandan marriage system.) Baskets also were used for ritual purposes, particularly to store and preserve masks. Many baskets were made to contain solid materials, and others were woven and closely coiled to hold liquids such as milk, which was used for rituals

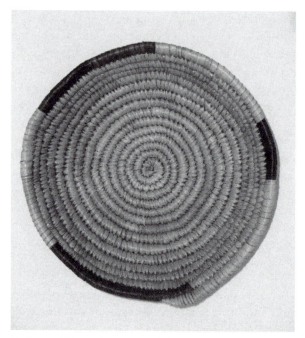

Basket making: A woven table mat. Courtesy of the author.

purposes. *Ikigega* baskets provide storage facilities, but they also serve as barns or granaries where food materials are stored. Successful farmers often possessed several *ikigega* because they had a good harvest. *Ikigega* could be installed in the house or within the enclosure. Winnowing baskets *(intara)* are used for cleaning or drying sorghum, maize, beans, or cassava flour. Big winnowing baskets were used as carpets to dry sorghum or maize, and small winnowing baskets served as plates.[10]

Basketry has not lost its cultural and economic importance in Rwanda. Although basket making does not yield a large income, there are efforts to revive the basket industry because it constitutes one of the ways to empower the women economically. Private and government-operated handicraft shops are located in large cities such as Kigali and Butare. The National Museum in Butare has a display of magnificent and elegant baskets. Basket making has become one of the cultural identities for Rwanda, past and present.

POTTERY

The Bantu-speaking people have been associated with the spread of iron technology and pottery in eastern Africa. They were particularly known for

their pottery called channeled ware, which were found in Rwanda. Archaeological excavations in central Rwanda reveal the presence of the Urewe
ceramics, which partly characterized the Bantu civilization.[11] In addition,
brick ironworking furnaces, which proved the highly sophisticated and
productive level of the Bantu pottery industry, were found in Rwanda.[12]
Given this evidence of archaeological connection, it is plausible to argue that
the Bantu people influenced the Rwandan potters, especially the Twa. In spite
of their small population, the Twa have been an important cultural part of
Rwanda, not only as hunters and dancers but also as traditional potters. Twa
and Bayovu women distinguished themselves in the traditional craft of
pottery. Girls learned the art at a very young age from their mothers and
gradually developed the skill. Pots of various sizes and designs were produced.
Like baskets, pots were made for household uses such as storing and serving
liquids and food. Pots, especially made by men, were also used for rituals.

Coil technique is used. Long strips of clay are made into coils and stacked
to form a pot. The shape of the pot was sometimes made by stacking the
coils around a mold. Decorations and patterns were placed on the pot before
it was fired.[13] Although the process took many hours, pot making did not
generate appreciable income. For example, "In 1984, a finished pot sold for
the Rwandan equivalent of about fifty U.S. cents."[14] In spite of the low
income derived from pottery, Rwandan women are still proud of their industry and creative ability.

To preserve and continue the tradition and to provide potters with economic
empowerment through commercialization, the Communauté des Autocthones
Rwandais (Community of Indigenous Peoples of Rwanda, CAURWA),
founded in 1995, established its Pottery Project in Kigali.[15] Although the seat
of CAURWA is located in Kigali, its activities span the whole country. One of
the objectives of the organization is to assist the marginalized Twa people by
providing them farming education, political awareness, and socioeconomic
opportunities for advancement. The organization also seeks to maintain Twa
traditions and culture. In accordance with its objectives, the organization has
promoted modern pottery, the business that is now witnessing a transformation.
The organization is encouraging and training Twa women on production and
marketing strategies. In addition to empowering the women, CAURWA is
also promoting Twa culture and customs through craftsmanship. Tourists are
patronizing the potters and basket makers. CAURWA works in collaboration
with world organizations and donors. The tide is now changing for the better
for the Twa people, who now participate more in Rwandan politics and
establish themselves in works of art and architecture.

The CAURWA Pottery Project is important to Twa women who face
problems of competition from the metal and plastic industries. In the wake

of industrialization, more durable and handy containers are being produced to replace old-fashioned pots. The Pottery Project, however, aims to enable women to maintain tradition and culture through appropriate and sustainable pottery technology and techniques.

ORNAMENTS

One of the hallmarks of the Rwandan culture is the making of ornaments. Rwandan women made hand-woven ornaments of various sizes and different designs. Palaces were decorated with artworks, and kings adorned themselves with beautiful ornaments. Particular reference has been made to Mazimpaka, who ruled the Nyiginya Kingdom between 1735 and 1756 and had natural physical beauty but often adorned himself with expensive ornaments. According to Jan Vansina, "Mazimpaka acquired a red bead from the East Coast that became a sensation."[16] Through interregional trade, glass beads from the East Coast became symbols of prestige and wealth in Rwanda. Hutu and Tutsi women adorn themselves with bead necklaces and bracelets.

Like other art industries, ornament making has not generated substantial income for Rwandan women. The poverty of many women increased in the aftermath of the 1994 genocide, and ornament making offered an alternative to return to normal life. Women weavers use their creative ability to send the message of peace and unity through the inscriptions on ornaments. For example, one inscription says *Agasozi kagufi kagushyikiriza akarekare* (Climbing even a short hill will bring us to a higher point). Ornaments include small baskets, table mats, and Christmas decorations. Tutsi women in particular were able to purchase and beautify themselves with expensive ornaments.

CONTEMPORARY ART FORMS

Tourists to Rwanda have discovered and admired the ingenuity of Rwandan artists. Many artwork patterns in basketry and pottery have not radically departed from the traditional styles, but contemporary artworks have become very attractive to foreigners. The impressive works of art from the rural areas include ceramics, basketry, traditional wood carvings, and paintings. Artworks, including masks of different sizes and shapes, are created and sold in the many open markets located in different cities. The Centre for the Formation of Arts Kigali has an extensive display of artworks.

Contemporary art is creating a new identity and a new focus. The beautiful two-color baskets with zigzag patterns have created an identity for Rwanda. The baskets have popularized Rwandan art, especially in the wake of the genocide. Blending traditional and modern materials, contemporary artists continue to use beads and cowrie shells in their works.

ARCHITECTURE AND TRADITIONAL HOUSING PATTERNS

Most Rwandans lived in close-knit rural and agricultural settlements where architecture had traditional expression. Houses were usually constructed on sites dictated by oracles. This religious dimension shows the reliance the Rwandan people placed on spirituality and ancestral worship. People resided in self-contained, small, beehive-style traditional huts, which were divided into sections and usually surrounded by cattle corrals. The circular, mud-wall buildings were arranged in compounds comprising lineage and clan members, which was the norm in many parts of Africa. Within the compounds, social life was predominately traditional.

Social events such as marriage ceremonies, entertainments, and relaxation activities were performed within the compounds. Archaeologists have unearthed remains of circular walls in Ryamurari, the old capital of the Ndorwa Kingdom, which suggests that the king's palace had an enclosure with cattle kraals built of cattle dung and garbage. Radiocarbon dates of the remains suggest that the walls were constructed between the eighteenth and twentieth centuries.[17] From the outside, the huts may look

Rwandan hut with tobacco leaves drying outside. Joan Batten/Art Directors & Trip Photo Library.

simple, but the internal structure was complex, allowing for family convenience and social activities. Children played freely in the compound and
were not prohibited from entering the huts of members of the extended
family. A typical Rwandan house was constructed as follows:

> Cypress poles with their ends buried in the ground, their tapering tops bent
> down to the centre and tied in place with concentric rings of reeds and bamboo.
> A circular ceiling, woven separately and propped in place before the poles are
> bent over, provides an inner layer. The exterior is thatched with overlapping
> bunches of grass tied to the outer frame rings with vegetable fibres.[18]

Family groups were scattered over the hills where their huts *(inzu)* were constructed in a circular enclosure, large enough to accommodate the livestock.
The enclosure and the house had a main entrance situated on the same axle.[19]

Huts were often small for poor families. Ashes enriched the soil of the enclosures, and banana plantations surrounded the family enclosure. Particularly in
central Rwanda, narrow bamboo panels were inserted to partition the hut or to
support the roof. The panels helped provide privacy. The location and size of the
rooms determined the height of the partitions. Unlike in central Rwanda, the
walls were larger in northern Rwanda. Beautiful bamboo baskets and ornaments
were used to decorate the huts. The size, the form of architectural design, the
type of decorations, the nature of the interior and exterior designs, and the
beauty of immediate surroundings distinguished the houses of poor and wealthy
families.[20] The construction of huts was exclusively the responsibility of the men
because women were, by custom, not allowed to go on the roof of the house.

Wealthy people built larger huts or houses with high and solid walls and
sanctuaries that were dedicated to the cult of the ancestors. Although dead, the
ancestors are believed to be part of the family and they are to be accorded high
honor. The traditional Tutsi hut *(u'rugo)* was the most important local architectural style because the Tutsi were wealthy cattle owners. Their houses were
complex, beautifully decorated, and well furnished. Most of the houses were
decorated with shields crossed with spears. Woven or beaded artifacts were hung
on the walls of the rooms. For example, many large houses were constructed in
Butare because it was the traditional seat of the Tutsi rulers. Also, the royal palace
at Nyanza was a huge building that was constructed entirely with traditional
materials. Today, the massive building serves as a national museum.

ARCHITECTURE AND MODERN HOUSING PATTERNS

The late nineteenth century witnessed the beginning of the construction
of modern buildings in the northern provinces of Gisenyi and Ruhengeri.

Modernization has dictated the fast-changing nature of architecture. Western-style buildings, especially government houses, are found in the main cities. Instead of grass-thatched roofs, corrugated iron sheets are now used. The Kigali Institute for Science, Technology and Management (KIST) has been established to promote urban planning and architecture. One of the most spectacular buildings is the National Museum in Butare, which displays spectacular Belgian architectural design. Butare is the capital of Rwandan culture, and many works of art and artifacts are found there. In the museum, room 5 has been specifically dedicated to the various aspects of Rwandan architecture, displaying the traditional living pattern and social organization of the people. In the center of the room is a reconstituted traditional hut. In this room, history has been reenacted.

Private houses in urban areas have borrowed Western-style architectural designs. Instead of the round architectural styles, houses are now constructed in rectangles with wooden windows. Concrete floors also have replaced decorated woven mats. Rwandans have imitated the styles and designs of houses of European missionaries and colonial officials but have incorporated indigenous Rwandan elements. The change in economic status as a result of business and investment ventures has had a positive impact on the patterns and designs of residential buildings. Many of the houses are in the bungalow format, but there are two-story buildings as well.

Houses on a Rwandan hillside. Howard Sayer/Art Directors & Trip Photo Library.

URBANIZATION

In the precolonial times, there was a limited degree of urbanization because most people lived in the rural areas where they pursued subsistence farming. The level of urbanization in Rwanda was the lowest in Africa (between 6% and 10%) because its economy was based exclusively on agriculture; therefore the population was essentially rural. Migration to urban centers such as Kigali was dictated by the search for employment in order to escape rural poverty. Declining conditions in agricultural production as a result of inadequate rainfall and lack of mechanized farming made movement to urban centers an attractive alternative. The increase in urban population has created some social problems such as poor housing and the rapid spread of diseases as a result of overcrowding among unskilled workers.

Successive governments since the colonial period have not seriously and effectively tackled the problem. Large towns such as Butare, Gisenyi, Gitarama, Kigali, and Nyabisindu were largely planned by the Belgians for economic purposes and administrative convenience. Foreigners such as Arabs, Belgians, Indians, and Pakistanis lived in the urban centers. The growth in population has encouraged rapid urbanization, which has created economic complications for the government. Hence, infrastructure is inadequate and economic opportunities very limited. Economic activities and the standard of living in the rural areas must be improved in order to allow people to stay instead of migrating to urban centers.

Studies in demography reveal that countries that have suffered civil wars, natural disasters, and political instability are susceptible to rapid urban growth. Returning refugees often settle in urban centers in order to have access to employment. This puts a strain on economic resources and social services provided by the government. Rwanda falls within this category. By 2002, the rate of urbanization had increase to approximately 16 percent, with the attendant problems of waste, poor sanitation, and water pollution. Kigali, the capital, is densely populated, and the increase in population became more apparent after the genocide. The problem will become more difficult to handle if soldiers are demobilized and settle in Kigali. To avoid overpopulation in the urban areas, the government has embarked on relocating people to the rural areas.

Access to sanitation remains low even in urban areas of Rwanda. In this respect, the government has been taking measures to enact housing policies that support healthful environmental conditions. The influx of migrants from rural to urban centers, the reintegration of refugees after the genocide, and the increase in the growth of foreigners have posed the challenge to the government to embark on appropriate housing in cities such as Kigali and

Butare. In order to decongest the urban areas, the government is not only pursuing a fundamental land reform but also attempting the relocation of most Rwandans into towns and villages. The so-called villagization policy carries the good intentions of providing better lives for the less privileged, encouraging agricultural growth, and developing commercial centers in rural areas while promoting business in the cities. A workshop on land use and villagization was held in Kigali in September 1999, and one of the recommendations was to provide guidelines on villagization, which "should include considerations of social structure to ensure the mixing of social groups and different generations, to allow for social growth and encourage the development of social skills and sustainable livelihoods."[21] The government is focusing on creating jobs and providing social amenities in the rural areas in order to check the influx to urban centers.

TECHNOLOGY

The development of indigenous industries and technology supported the Rwandan economy in the precolonial period. Traditional methods were utilized in the manufacturing of farming implements such as hoes, diggers, knives, and machetes, which were used in the cultivation of food crops. The country had no well-developed farming technology, no extensive harvest technology, and no preservative and storage facilities.

Modern technology is gradually revolutionizing the Rwandan economy. New technologies have replaced traditional ones, and they reduce the cost of production and increase the volume of production. The poor people in the rural areas are gaining access to manufactured goods produced in Rwanda.

The government is formulating policies that will increase the technological growth of the country. By promoting information and communication technology, the government is shifting from the traditional agricultural system to an economy based on modern technology. Multinational corporations are supporting technological initiatives and the transfer of technology. In this age of information and communication technology, Rwanda is taking every advantage to encourage the youth to embrace technology. In Kigali, the Institute of Science, Technology and Management has expanded its curriculum to include computer technology in order to contribute to nation growth and development, and the government has cooperated with India on technology exchange.

A significant improvement has been made in the art and architecture of Rwanda. Indigenous Rwandans as well as foreign artists are using modern technology to bring about changes in artwork. Women who were not making substantial income through basketry and pottery are being encouraged and supported by international organizations. Rwanda is receiving worldwide attention through artworks, which portray the traditional culture and customs of the country.

Urbanization is also changing the landscape of Rwanda. Major cities in the beautiful country of many hills are rapidly increasing in population, and modern houses and spectacular architectural designs are the result. Government and private houses are being constructed with materials from the industrial world, without completely displacing traditional architectural designs.

NOTES

1. Lynn Mackenzie, *Non-Western Art: A Brief Guide,* 2nd ed. (Upper Saddle River, NJ: Prentice Hall, 2001), 7.

2. Jan Vansina, *Antecedents to Modern Rwanda: The Nyiginya Kingdom* (Madison: University of Wisconsin Press, 2004), 63.

3. Glenn E. King, *Traditional Cultures: A Survey of Nonwestern Experience and Achievement* (Prospect Heights, IL: Waveland Press, 2003), 200.

4. Muhereza Kyamutetera, "Discovering Rwanda's Sights and Sounds," *Daily Monitor,* n.d., http://www.monitor.co.ug/specialincludes/mplsups/rwandaecon/econ09195.php.

5. "The Pulse of Africa," BBC World Service, August 2004, http://news.bbc.co.uk/nol/shared/bsp/hi/pdfs/18_10_04_pulse.pdf, 17.

6. Epaphrodite Binamungu has distinguished himself as a great sculptor. He has organized exhibitions in the Democratic Republic of the Congo, France, Uganda, Rwanda, Switzerland, and the United States. He co-owns the Enganzo Art Gallery in Kigali with another Rwandan artist.

7. "Mary Cassatt (1844–1926)," Art History on Stamps, 2006, http://arthistory.heindorffhus.dk/frame-MaryCassatt.htm.

8. "Lidded Basket [Rwanda; Tutsi people] (1978.412.327a,b)." In *Timeline of Art History* (New York: Metropolitan Museum of Art, 2000), October 2006, http://www.metmuseum.org/toah/ho/11/sfe/hod_1978.412.327a,b.htm.

9. Rene S. Wassing, *African Art: Its Background and Traditions* (New York: Konecky and Konecky, 1968), 51.

10. These materials can be found in the National Museum in Butare.

11. Vansina, *Antecedents to Modern Rwanda,* 18.

12. J.E.G. Sutton, "East Africa before the Seventh Century," in *General History of Africa. Vol. 2: Ancient Civilizations of Africa,* ed. G. Mokhtar (Berkeley, CA: Heinemann Educational Books, UNESCO, 1981), 582.

13. Jerome Lewis and Judy Knight, *The Twa of Rwanda* (Copenhagen, Denmark: World Rainforest Movement, International Work Group of Indigenous Affairs and Survival International (France), 1995).

14. Christopher Taylor, *Milk, Honey and Money: Changing Concepts in Rwandan Healing* (Washington, DC: Smithsonian Institution Press, 1992), 16.

15. CAURWA is the largest indigenous network in Rwanda. It is a nongovern-mental organization that supports the Twa through income-generating projects.

16. Vansina, *Antecedents to Modern Rwanda,* 83.

17. F. L. Van Noten, "The Iron Age in the North and East," in *The Archaeology of Central Africa,* ed. F. L. Van Noten (Graz, Austria: Akademische Druck- und Ver-lagsanstalt, 1982), 69–76.

18. Robin Kent, "Conservation in Rwanda," Robin Kent Architecture and Conservation, 2006, http://www.robinkent.com/rwanda/articles_rwanda.html.

19. "Habitat," The Rwandan National Museum, n.d. http://www.museum.gov.rw/2_museums/butare/pages_html/intro/page_intro.htm.

20. Ibid.

21. Robin Palmer, "Report on the Workshop on Land use and Villagisation in Rwanda," Oxfam, 1999, http://www.oxfam.org.uk/what_we_do/issues/livelihoods/landrights/downloads/kigali.rtf.

5

Cuisine and Traditional Dress

An empty stomach can make a person lose his or her cattle.

—African proverb

Tell me what you eat, and I'll tell you who you are.

—Jean Anthelme Brillat-Savarin, 1825

Although eating is a biological necessity, food is an integral part of a society's culture. The society determines what can be eaten, the method of preparation, and eating ethics. Societies have different kinds of food, different lifestyles, and different eating habits. These are determined largely by the culture and are based on ethnic, social, and religious background. Rwandan cuisine is a reflection of the people's occupational and ethnosocial classification. As there are regular daily foods, there also are different meals for specific social and religious celebrations. Unlike food, dress has not been determined by ethnic affiliation but essentially by gender and royalty. Clothes were specifically designed for the kings and others generally worn by commoners. The trend in modern Rwanda is illustrated by an African proverb, "When the drumbeat changes, the dance changes." The cuisine and dressing styles in Rwanda are changing with time and with external influence.

CUISINE

Since precolonial times, Rwandans had been engaged in a subsistence-level agricultural economy. In this traditional economic system, people produced only what they consumed without offering any of their products for sale because they usually had no surplus to sell. To a large extent, this subsistence economic system determined their consumption and dietary culture. The Hutu and Twa in particular were low-income farmers and hunters. Accordingly, their staple foods consisted of roots, tubers, bananas, plantains, and pulses. Because they were agrarian people, they were able to eat more solid foods compared to the Tutsi pastoralists who fed mainly on milk and other dairy products. Other foods the Hutu and Twa consumed included beans, corn, millet, peas, sweet potatoes, cassava, and fruits such as avocados, mangos, and papayas. They also ate vegetables such as spinach. Due to a diet low in meat consumption, they were deficient in certain proteins and minerals usually provided in animal products. Although they had cattle, the animals served primarily as symbols of wealth and status rather than as a source of food. Many people consumed meat only about twice a month. Only those individuals who lived near lakes ate fish, in particular tilapia. A great number of Rwandans were unable to diversify their diets with vegetables and other vitamin-rich foods because of lack of financial resources and job opportunities. Rwandans experienced a rapid increase in diseases caused by vitamin deficiency, especially among children.

A majority of the people ate twice a day, having sweet potatoes and porridge (consisting of a mixture of sorghum, corn, millet, and milk) for breakfast and boiled beans, bananas, sweet potatoes, or cassava for lunch. Sweet potatoes can be boiled, fried, or roasted and remain a primary high-energy food. Approximately 90 percent of the population consumes them on a regular basis. The planting season for sorghum falls between December and February, but low rainfall often leads to a poor harvest. Believed to have been introduced by Germans and Belgian missionaries, potatoes became an important part of the Rwandan diet.[1] Potatoes can be eaten fresh or dried and are cultivated on a large scale in Gitarama and Butare. Historically, the Butare region has been known to be the largest producer of sweet potatoes, beans, sorghum, groundnuts, and manioc. Kibuye has been a producer of potatoes and peas. Byumba also produces sorghum, and Gitarama produces manioc, sweet potatoes, taro, beans, and bananas.

Introduced into Rwanda from Uganda between the sixteenth and seventeenth centuries, beans, as the main legume, are planted by many farmers in rural areas and have brought about profound social and dietary changes among the people of Rwanda. Israel Ntaganzwa-Rugamba asserted that "since they were first introduced, beans are by far the most consumed food in the country."[2] Although their consumption increases the amount of protein in the people's diet and improves their nutritional intake, beans are not produced in large enough quantities. Additionally, a drop in their price often produces negative economic consequences for their farmers. Maize (corn) is another important staple that is heavily consumed by Rwandans. Like beans, maize is not produced in large quantities and sometimes has to be imported from Uganda.

The top cash and food crops in Rwanda are bananas and plantains. By the fifteenth century, as a result of commercial interactions with the Swahili states of East Africa, bananas had been introduced from China and Indonesia to Rwanda by way of the Indian Ocean. They are grown year-round by small-scale farmers. Banana consumption in Rwanda is one of the highest in the world.[3] According to reports from the Food and Agriculture Organization, "Bananas and plantains are traditionally preserved by drying or fermenting the dried products and, in particular, flour being the most important nutritionally, although beer is also a major product in Uganda and Rwanda where the utilization of green bananas is particularly high."[4] Because they receive moderate rainfall throughout the year, prefectures such as Cyangugu, Gisenyi, Kibuye, Kibungo, and Kigali are the traditional banana producers. Everywhere across the country, bananas also are used for brewing beer as well as for cooking. They also provide a small income for the growers. Cheaper sources of food are purchased from the proceeds of the sale of banana beer. Plantain grows under similar conditions as bananas and when ripe can be eaten fresh or made into *mizuzu* (fried plantains).

Maize, a major cereal food crop, which is increasingly popular, was introduced into Rwanda in the eighteenth century. Because their conditions for growth are similar, maize is usually planted twice a year and may be intercropped with beans. The nutritional importance of maize lies in the high quantity of carbohydrates it provides and the proteins it supplies to the population.[5] Boiled and roasted maize are sold by women.

Since its introduction to Rwanda in 1930 by the Belgians, cassava has been the main source of calories, one of the principal staple foods, and the third most consumed food after bananas and sweet potatoes. Cassava, a tuberous and drought-resistant crop, does not require frequent weeding and grows faster than other crops because it can be harvested in six months. Both the roots and leaves of the cassava plant are edible.

Cassava is intercropped with bananas, beans, and maize, but surplus production yields little income to rural small-scale farmers. Although planted all over the country, cassava is the main crop in Gitarama and Gikonko. The absence of mechanized farming and irregular rainfall militates against large production. In producing, harvesting, processing, and marketing cassava, both women and male youth play a significant role.

The Portuguese introduced cassava to Africa after they found it growing in Brazil. Cassava is a tropical crop, which has the ability to thrive in different soil types and can remain in the soil for a long time before it is harvested.

Therefore, it is a good famine-prevention crop. When ripe and harvested, cassava can be eaten raw without being processed. It is a low-fat food and can be processed into chips or powdery starch through traditional and labor-intensive methods, which include peeling the skin, fermentation, and drying. Foods made with cassava include bread, *umutsima* (a dish of corn pasta), and *isombe* (cassava leaves) with eggplant and spinach.[6]

Rice is heavily consumed, especially in the urban centers, but its production is limited. Varieties of rice are imported into Rwanda for three reasons: there is increasing demand, locally produced rice is expensive, and foreign-produced rice is of higher quality. Rice is often boiled before being eaten in a stew or mixed with beans. Besides serving as a daily staple food, rice also serves as a ceremonial food. During social occasions or ceremonies, rice is often served. To increase rice production and ease food shortages, the Rwandan government has allowed agronomists from Taiwan and China to attempt to cultivate rice on a large scale.

MEAT AND MILK

Rwandans have experienced numerous health problems essentially because of a lack of protein in their diets. Unlike in the urban centers, where goats, beef, and chicken were consumed, people in the rural areas did not eat meat or drink milk on a regular basis. This was because cattle (seen as a sign of wealth and status) were not often slaughtered for meat. Goats, introduced from neighboring countries, were domesticated and usually provided a healthy diet and income for their owners. Although sheep were domesticated, a religious taboo prohibited the eating of lamb, though sheepskin was used for clothing.

Animal husbandry was an integral part of the Rwandan culture for many centuries. Cattle, especially, served as a symbol of political power and were the traditional mainstay of the Rwandan economy. The importance of cattle in the Rwandan society is demonstrated in the proverb *ushaka inka arara nkazo* (He who seeks to obtain cattle is made to sleep outdoor like them).[7] Cattle also contributed significantly to the diet of the people. The consumption of milk and dairy products (mainly from cattle) was important to the health of the people of Rwanda. The production of milk and butter was carried out by a process of fermentation with the use of traditional technology. Milk serves two primary functions: "as a therapeutic weapon to combat against acidic toxicity" and as "a good source of nutrients that has a high biological nutritional value for children, old men and feeding patients."[8]

The Tutsi's diet consisted of more liquid than solid food. Milk, in particular, was central to their diet because as pastoralists, "They had access to milk and the various alcoholic beverages."[9] Occasionally, they ate beef and solid vegetable foods. Unlike the Tutsi, the Hutu consumed grains, vegetable food-stuffs, and goat meat, and the Twa ate almost every type of food and meat. Following this hierarchy of consumption, it becomes apparent that people at the lower level of the social order ate more solid foods, whereas the privileged upper class consumed more liquid foods and beverages.

UBUDEHE: COLLECTIVE WORK

Ubudehe, a traditional Rwandan practice of collective cooperative work, portrays a sense of unity and togetherness primarily for economic purposes. The Rwandans adopted the cultural practice of *ubudehe* as a mechanism of working in groups and teams. This system promotes and strengthens socio-economic relationships between members of the community. In the traditional system, *ubudehe* is practiced at two levels—family and community—as a form of economic empowerment and a means of fighting poverty, especially among the rural population. Rooted in cultural form of solidarity, both men and women participated in *ubudehe,* which involved the digging of fields before the rains along with the planting and the harvesting of crops.[10] Because the system had always been a useful and effective traditional source of assistance, the government has revived it to serve "as a model for a program designed to alleviate poverty and provide for community rebuilding in the wake of the Rwandan genocide and civil war in the early 1990s."[11]

In the Rwandan culture, a woman's work was usually harder than a man's. Women's responsibilities included cleaning the house, cooking, fetching water from the river or stream, caring for children, cultivating the land, harvesting crops, and pounding grain into flour. Though very time-consuming, the pounding of grain into flour for household consumption brought in little income if sold. Women learned to support each other by forming cooperative associations to work on fellow members' fields.

BEVERAGES

Beer and milk are important beverages. Beer was consumed as a beverage in social and religious ceremonies such as marriages and divination rituals. As hospitable people, Rwandans offered beer to their guests. Drunkenness was commonplace, and the Hutu even have beer-drinking songs.[12] Many people brewed their own beer and alcoholic beverages from bananas or dry sorghum through a fermentation process. An alcoholic drink brewed from dry sorghum is known as *ikigage* and is believed to have medicinal powers. The women squeeze bananas by hand, using handfuls of hard grasses, and the juice is filtered into jars. Roasted sorghum flour is added to the banana juice and the mixture left to ferment for one to two days, after which the beer (known as *urwagwa*) is ready for drinking.[13] *Urwagwa* is cheap and can be intoxicating. Women seldom drink alcohol, but men frequently drink beer with straws from a single large container.[14]

Although coffee was not consumed in large quantities by Rwandans themselves, it was widely cultivated in the rural areas but generated little income. Coffee, especially the traditional arabica Bourbon variety, is cultivated in prefectures such as Cyangugu, Gisenyi, Gikongoro, Gitarama, Kibungo, and Kigali. The large-scale cultivation of coffee has been affected by occasional droughts, crop diseases, and fluctuations in the price of coffee on the world markets. Coffee has become a major export crop, and the U.S. coffee chain Starbucks has purchased Rwandan coffee.[15] The quality of Rwandan coffee has been steadily improving, and its cultivation and sale is helping sustain the income for small-scale coffee growers. With financial, technical, and logistic assistance from international organizations, the coffee industry is rapidly improving in Rwanda.[16] Rwandans make healthful nonalcoholic beverages out of fruits, but they do not meet international standard for exportation.

UNDERLYING REASONS FOR THE FOOD CRISIS

Successive governments in Rwanda have struggled to develop mechanisms for sustainable agricultural production; however, there have been no sufficient incentives for small farmers to expand their production. The result from this problem has been a gross shortage of food.[17] Due to several factors, Rwanda has experienced food crises for many years. First, land available for food production is limited. Known as the Land of a Thousand Hills and the Land of Gorillas, much of Rwanda is covered by a mountainous terrain and has much wildlife, and a greater part of the land has been overcultivated. Many farmers still survive on their ancestral smallholdings, which is rotated from year to year. According to a recent study, Rwandan farming techniques have come into question:

> Farmland is severely depleted of the basic nutrients needed to grow crops.... Traditionally, farmers cleared land, grew crops for a few harvests, then let it fallow for 10 or 15 years to rejuvenate as they moved on to clear more land.... But as they try to feed a rapidly growing population, the farmers instead grow crop after crop, sapping the soil's fertility.[18]

In desperate need of more farmland, Rwandans have increased deforestation.[19] The clearing of forests further enables wind and rain to blow away vitally needed topsoil, preventing good harvests.[20] In precolonial times, fertilizer was unknown, but diviners, on behalf of the king, usually performed rituals to restore the fertility to the land and to prevent harvesting calamities. During and after the colonial period, fertilizer, which could restore productivity, was very expensive and unaffordable by Rwanda's small-scale farmers. In addition, the pasturing of cattle took away farmland. As well, small farm landholdings, especially around the Virunga Mountains, do not permit mechanized forms of agriculture because tractors cannot be used effectively on fragmented farmlands.

Second, farmers have a lack of adequate farming tools and techniques. Traditional hoes and diggers are not adequate for large-scale food production. Third, the population is growing faster than food production. Rwanda is the most densely populated country in Africa, and its land and farming mechanisms do not provide a strong agricultural base. Fourth, erratic rainfall has a devastating impact on agricultural production, resulting in droughts, poor harvests, famines, and malnourishment. Rwanda experienced a series of famines during the period of worldwide economic depression in the 1930s. During World War II, another devastating famine forced many people to migrate out of the country. The countries in East Africa where they went, such as Ethiopia, Mozambique, and Somalia, also experience drought and food crises from time to time. Fifth, frequent ethnic conflicts, civil strife, and political instabilities have forced many people out of the country, further reducing the labor force available for food production.

In the recent postgenocide period, the issue of displaced refugees also has had a negative impact on food production. Demographic movements and insecurity, especially in the northwestern part of the country, diminish the levels of food production. In addition, the increasing number of HIV patients has significantly lowered the number of adult workers available to work in the fields. These conditions have forced Rwanda to import food or depend on international aid to alleviate the food shortage. On a positive note, intensified efforts within Rwanda, with the assistance of international relief organizations, not only replenish but also retain quality soil and in turn produce larger yields of more nutritious crops.

FOOD, GIFTS, AND CEREMONIES

Over much of sub-Saharan Africa in precolonial times, gift-giving was a customary practice and a social ideology. Men particularly were expected to offer gifts to relations on specified occasions or during special ceremonies. Gift-giving facilitated the egalitarian ethos of the culture.[21] In Rwanda, as in many parts of Africa, food constituted a major portion of the gifts offered to relatives and friends during social and religious ceremonies and included food, cow, and liquid gifts. Food, in particular, was employed "as a symbol in issues related to social and biological reproduction."[22] Christopher Taylor explains the spirit of sharing and gift-giving in Rwanda by stating that "after the period of seclusion *(ikilili)* that follows the birth of a new child, people bring different kinds of food and other gifts to the new mother. The wife's parents bring a quantity of sorghum porridge in thought to stimulate the production of breast milk." He also pointed out that "the gift of cow is more significant than the gift of alcoholic beverages, which in turn are more significant than the gift of solid foodstuffs."[23]

With the assistance of the *abiru,* the *mwami* performed a series of rituals in which food and liquids formed a principal part. In their examination of the royal rituals in ancient Rwanda, d'Hertefelt and Coupez indicated that milk was used in most of the performances.[24] In addition to milk, sorghum and honeyed sorghum beer also were used in royal rituals, and bean cakes were especially important in local ceremonies.

MODERN DIET

In 1965, the World Bank rated Rwanda as the most malnourished nation. Since then, however, efforts by individuals and governments geared toward improving the dietary culture of the people have been started. Roasted corn and plantains and barbecued meat are only some of the modern foods that vendors sell in urban areas. In order to produce a greater diversity of crops and for the people to eat a more healthful and balanced diet, various organizations provide agricultural training to the youth.

Beans are household food, and their consumption is increasing because they are an essential source of protein. In recent years, farmers have been able to grow different varieties of beans during the two growing seasons of the year. Along with coffee, beans also have become cash crops. Sweet potatoes, along with sorghum and rice, also make up the common, everyday diet of Rwandans. The cultivation of sweet potatoes has intensified based on the high demand.

To accommodate the increasing number of tourists to Rwanda, the cuisine has remarkably changed. Hotels and restaurants serve both Western and local foods. For example, in many restaurants local modern foods include goat meat kebabs, grilled or fried fish, and stews usually consisting of beans or meat. Side dishes often include *ubugali* (cassava meal), *matoke* (cooked banana or plantain), boiled potatoes, or rice. Legend states that Kintu, the first man on earth, brought *matoke* to Uganda, and from there it spread to Rwanda and Tanzania. Chez Mama Manzi is one of the small restaurants where traditional foods, such as *igisafuriya* (a goat and banana dish with peanut stew made in restaurants), are served. Rwandan restaurants also serve foods found in almost any U.S. or European restaurant, such as French fries, chicken, fish, and steak served with rice or potatoes.

TRADITIONAL DRESS

Clothing

Clothing has been part of human culture since prehistoric times. The form of clothes or dress may differ from society to society, but generally clothes are worn for modesty and to protect the body from environmental hazards. Clothing also can be used as a symbol of prestige or identity. For example, the type of clothes worn by rulers or wealthy people usually differs from that by the common folk. In any given society, religious regulations, economic structure, culture, tradition, as well as way of life influence the clothing that people wear.[25] The evolution of clothing from leaves and tree bark to fabrics has a long history. The weaving of fabric has been dated to 8000 B.C., at the beginning of the Neolithic era.[26] In her article on clothing, Valerie Steele indicated:

> The production of textiles requires the ability to process fibres, spin them into thread, and make cloth from the thread. Cloth can be made in a variety of ways, such as knotting, knitting, and braiding, but most cloth is made by weaving. Weaving is usually done on a loom that holds long threads (called the warp) under uniform tension so that other threads (the wool or weft) can be inserted over and under them.[27]

Rwandan people, like other societies, went through a process of change in cloth making and in dressing.

Clothes of Bark

Before fabrics were developed, the people of Rwanda, like many other societies in the world, used plant products or skins as their clothing. To turn bark into cloth involved a long process, beginning with the obtainment of bark from the *imivumu* (ficus tree), using pruning and slashing knives. The bark was hammered and pounded until it became soft, and then it was twisted, squeezed, and smoothened with an *imangu* (wooden tool) until it was flexible and clothlike. Sometimes, decorations of different colors and patterns embellished the fabric. Clothes also were made from banana tree bark. Tailors assembled, cut into pieces, and then sewed together the fabrics from bark or banana trees to make garments, mostly loincloths, for children and adult men and women. The use

Rwandan woman walking with goods. Howard Sayer/Art Directors & Trip Photo Library.

of bark for clothing diminished during the early part of the twentieth century and completely disappeared after World War II.[28]

Clothes of Skins

For many centuries, the skin of cows, calves, and goats were used for clothing. The skin usually was beaten with sticks, the hair removed, and then spread in the sun for about two days. Soaked in water to soften and later stretched between poles, the skin was scraped with an *imbazo* (scraper) to remove the flesh. Grease was rubbed on the skin to make it smooth. It was then cut, assembled, and stitched. Married women wore a loincloth called *inkanda*. It could be worn with or without a plaited belt made of cowhide.[29]

Goat skin also was used for clothing, especially by young boys and girls. The *ishabure* is a short goat-skin loincloth with elaborate, colorful, and beautiful designs and was worn by girls around their hips or fixed on their shoulder. Goat skin is most commonly used for capes, which covered the upper part of the body and one shoulder. Wealthy people displayed their wealth by wearing capes made of antelope skin, and priests wore capes made of either wildcat or monkey skin while conducting rites of the traditional cult called *kubandwa*. Belts were worn by men and women to hold either the *inkanda* or the *ishabure*. A belt also could serve as a symbol of affection if it was passed from a mother-in-law to her newly married daughter-in-law.[30] Today, hides and skin generate a substantial foreign exchange for the Rwandan government as the country's fourth largest export.

ADORNMENTS

Men and women adorned themselves in many ways. Adornment may be in the form of jewelry such as bracelets, necklaces, and earrings. It may be armlets, belts, bracelets, and pendants. In many African societies, beads, brass, gold, ivory, and leather have been used to make beautiful jewelry. Feathers, particularly ostrich feathers, also have been part of African adornment.

Personal adornment may be in the form of hairstyles or body decorations such as tattoos. Adornment could be artistic or could depict the social status and wealth of the individual. Some jewelry was worn for religious purposes, and expensive ones were primarily for reasons of prestige. Rwandans loved to adorn themselves, not only for the aesthetic appeal or enhancement of their own personal beauty but also for social and celebratory reasons. Different kinds of jewelry were worn as part of the traditional daily dress or during ritual ceremonies. Women adorned themselves with well-crafted beads, bracelets, earrings, necklaces, and rings. In addition, women wore beautiful hair styles decorated with beads or different ornaments. The Tutsi women were well known for their adherence to elaborate traditional methods of personal adornment.

ROYAL DRESS

Rwandan kings dressed elaborately and flamboyantly, as expected of their position. Early Rwandan rulers often dressed in royal garments of leopard skin and sandals. Part of their paraphernalia included a ring, tools, vestments, and royal drums.

Royal clothing and adornment were special, including beaded crown or special headgear, which symbolized royalty and power. Wearing of crowns by kings was a prevalent part of African culture. The royal headdress, called *igisingo,* consisted of "a bonnet entirely covered with beads, the fringes in front falling on the face, with varied density."[31] The presence of beads, especially in Gitarama, suggests that Rwanda established commercial relations with Arab, Indian, or Nyamwezi merchants along the east coast or participated in the transatlantic trade. Kings wore beaded crowns on special occasions, as during the installation ceremony of a new king. Diviners also used beads on their divination dish boards.

Since a republic was proclaimed in Rwanda, all the vestiges of nobility, including royal dressing, have been wiped out. All the paraphernalia of the king, including the royal drums, which were traditionally venerated and sprinkled with the blood of bull calves, no longer command respect. The Western political system and Western modes of dress have replaced the old monarchical and ceremonial practices. In government offices and in official ceremonies, Rwandans now dress in Western fashions.

DANCING DRESS

Dancing has been one of the important social and cultural activities of the Rwandan people for many centuries. Each dance has its own special costumes. The *intore* dance, for example, is an ancient warrior dance, which used to be performed to celebrate victory in wars. Dancers used to perform exclusively for the king in the palace, but today, dancers are based in Butare, where the National Museum is located, and perform for all, especially for tourists. The splendid and colorful costume of the dancers consists of long or short skirts, ankle belts, and headbands made of different beads, headdresses with grass wigs, small hand-painted shields, and sticks, which represent spears.

The Inganzo Ballet is a dance troupe whose members wear long skirts with beaded belts worn across their chest and bells attached to their ankles. On their own part, the *tambourinaires* (drummers) wear short skirts and beaded belts across their chest and shoulders.

WESTERN INFLUENCE

In several ways, Rwandan culture is changing in regard to food and dress due to the proliferation of people from the Western world. Colonialism brought the Germans and Belgians to Rwanda, but more Europeans penetrated the country after the recent genocide. The presence of the Europeans has engendered profound change through the introduction and adoption of the Western style of dress. Unlike in Zaire where Sese Seko Mobutu outlawed Western styles in order to promote traditional values, after independence in 1962, the government of Rwanda encouraged and required the people to wear Western-style clothing. In many Rwandan cities such as Kigali and Butare, people dress in the Western fashion for daily wear but on special occasions and holidays wear their traditional garments. The influx of Western tourists and journalists, as well as those who belong to various humanitarian, religious, and political world organizations, is forcing Rwandans to adopt new styles of dress in schools, offices, and social gatherings.[32] Young city dwellers are adapting particularly well to the Western way of dressing. In spite of the increasing Western influences, Rwandan food and dress culture and customs continue to persist, and it will be difficult to completely displace them, particularly in the rural areas where foreign impact is less felt.

Rwanda is one of the countries in tropical Africa in which more than half of the labor force is engaged in agriculture, producing food crops with traditional farming methods. The traditional and primitive farming mechanisms and practices, used for centuries, have not changed significantly because of a limited exposure to new technologies and techniques as well as economic constraints. Most of the Rwandan population live and work in rural areas, but fertile volcanic soils attract dense settlements.[33] Traditional differences in political, economic, and social status reflect in the dietary patterns of the Rwandan people. Rwanda, like many other African countries, is facing the challenges of increasing food production to meet the ever-increasing rise in population. The rate of poverty and starvation will continue unless a substantial increase in food production can occur. Owing to poor diet and a lack of an adequate water supply, many people, especially foreigners, come down with food- and waterborne diseases. Increasing storage facilities and techniques will help in the preservation of food and reduce food shortages.

The rapid change in the mode of dress associated primarily with modernization. Although bark and skins are no longer used for clothing, traditional ways of dressing are not completely displaced. Royal dressing no longer exists because of the abolition of kingship. Traditional dressing, however, as reflected in the dance dress of the *intore* and the Inganzo Ballet, continues to persevere. Western influences and new fashions can be seen as a result of increasing interaction between Rwanda and the outside world.

NOTES

1. G. Durr, *Potato Production and Utilization in Rwanda* (Lima, Peru: International Potato Center, 1983).

2. Israel Ntaganzwa-Rugamba, "A Classic Colonial Distortion of African History and Its Catastrophic Consequences," January 2000, http://users.skynet.be/wirira/rwandais.htm.

3. "Banana Program," ATDT Project: Rwanda, n.d., http://www.isar.cgiar.org/atdt/banana/banana.htm.

4. Pamela A. Lancaster and D. G. Coursey, *Traditional Post-harvest Technology of Perishable Tropical Staples* (Tropical Development and Research Institute, FAO Agricultural Services Bulletin, Rome, no. 59, 1984), 46.

5. Ibid.

6. Directions for preparing *isombe:* Boil cassava leaves until tender. Add chopped green onions, eggplant, spinach, and green peppers. Cook on medium heat for 10 minutes. Add palm oil and peanut butter. Simmer for 10 minutes, stirring occasionally, Serve with rice or bread. Ingredients: 2 bunches cassava leaves, washed and chopped (another leafy vegetable may be substituted); 2 green onions, chopped; 2 medium eggplants, cut into chunks; 2 packages spinach, washed and chopped; 2 green peppers, sliced into pieces; 3 tablespoons palm oil; 3 tablespoons peanut butter. "Eating the Rwandan Way," n.d., http://www.cp-pc.ca/english/rwanda/eating.html.

7. Ntaganzwa-Rugamba, "A Classic Colonial Distortion of African History."

8. François Dominicus Nzabuheraheza, "Milk Production and Hygiene in Rwanda," *AJFAND* Online 5, no. 2 (2005), http://www.ajfand.net/Issue-IX-files/IssueIX-commentary.htm.

9. Christopher Taylor, *Milk, Honey and Money: Changing Concepts in Rwandan Healing* (Washington, DC: Smithsonian Institution Press, 1992), 38.

10. The concept of *ubudehe* cut across ethnic affiliation, but it was directed to providing financial assistance through self-help and collaborative works. It was mainly for farmwork but not limited to it. *Ubudehe* "also extended to those who are too poor or incapacitated to take part in the collective action. After the group has completed their fields they move on to the fields of those who have not been able to participate directly. A successful harvest is then celebrated with *umuganura* made from collecting together donations from everyone's first harvest." Ministry of Finance and Economic Planning, Republic of Rwanda, "Ubudehe to Fight Poverty," http://www.eurodad.org/uploadstore/cms/docs/ubudehe.doc.

11. Judith Dunbar, "Ubudehe and the Kecamatan Development Projects: Case Study and Comparative Analysis" (master's thesis, Tufts University, 2004); République Rwandaise, Ministère des Finances et de la Planification Economique, "Ubudehe mu Kurwanya Ubukene" (Kigali, Rwanda: Ministry of Finance and Economic Planning, April 2, 2003).

12. Alan P. Merriam, *African Music in Perspective* (New York: Garland, 1982), 68.

13. Lancaster and Coursey, *Traditional Post-Harvest Technology,* 47.

14. "Food in Rwanda," World Investment News, 2003, http://www.winne.com/rwanda/bf13.html.

15. Orla Ryan, "Rwanda's Struggle to Rebuild Economy," BBC News, April 1, 2004, http://news.bbc.co.uk/1/hi/business/3586851.stm.

16. Tracy Ging, "The Healing Effect of Coffee in Rwanda," *News and Resources,* http://www.coffeeinstitute.org/news.asp?id=15.

17. Joachim von Braun, Hartwig De Haen, and Juergen Blanken, *Commercialization of Agriculture under Population Pressure: Effects on Production, Consumption, and Nutrition in Rwanda* (Washington, DC: International Food Policy Research Institute, Research Report 85, 1991), 15.

18. Celia W. Dugger, "Overfarming African Land Is Worsening Hunger Crisis," *The New York Times,* March 31, 2006, A7.

19. Rwanda-Intensified Land Use Management Project in the Buberuke Highlands in Ruhondo district trains and helps in planting of trees in order to prevent deforestation

and continued erosion of soil. "IFAD through Photography," IFAD, n.d., http://www.ifad.org/photo/region/PF/RW.htm.

20. Ibid.

21. For the social ideology of gift-giving in West Africa, see Julius O. Adekunle, *Politics and Society in Nigeria's Middle Belt: Borgu and the Emergence of a Political Identity* (Trenton, NJ: Africa World Press, 2004), 162ff.

22. Ibid., 6.

23. Taylor, *Milk, Honey and Money,* 5–6.

24. M. d'Hertefelt and A. Coupez, *La royauté sacrée de l'ancien Rwanda* (Tervuren, Belgium: Musée Royal de l'Afrique Centrale, Annales Sciences Humaines, no. 52, 1964).

25. Valerie Steele, "Clothing," Microsoft Encarta Online Encyclopedia, 2006, http://Encarta.msn.com/text_761569657_1/Clothing.html.

26. Ibid.

27. Ibid.

28. "Clothing, Jewelry and Leisure," Rwandan National Museum, n.d., http://www.museum.gov.rw/2_museums/butare/pages_html/room_6/text_clothing_jewelry_leisure.htm.

29. Ibid.

30. Ibid.

31. Ibid.

32. Veronique Tadjo, *The Shadow of Imana: Travels in the Heart of Rwanda,* trans. Véronique Wakerley (Johannesburg, South Africa: Heinemann, 2002).

33. Tony Binns, *Tropical Africa* (New York, Routledge, 1994), 13, 29.

6

Gender Roles, Marriage, and Family

People helping one another can bring an elephant into the house.
—Rwandan proverb

Social institutions provide a framework that guides the relationships of people and constitutes the bedrock of the culture and customs in a society. In Rwanda, the institutions of marriage, family, and kinship developed over a long period of time. These institutions ensure the continuity of the people's culture and customs by passing them from one generation to the next. The close relationship between family, clan, and lineage members laid a solid background for the culture and traditions of Rwanda to survive and thrive as well as adapt to changes and challenges. Many factors influenced the social institutions and gender roles in Rwanda. The key ones include urbanization, colonialism, independence, modernization, and Western education. Since independence, government policies have either influenced or altered traditional marriage, family structure, and gender division within the labor force. In the 1970s, the scarcity of land forced people to migrate from the provinces of Gikongoro, Gisenyi, Kibuye, and Ruhengeri to the eastern and central regions of Rwanda.[1]

Christianity along with Western culture and Western education are the driving forces behind the gradual shift from polygynous to monogamous marriages. The more Rwandans become educated, the more they embrace monogamy and small families. Prearranged or forced marriages are diminishing as the young people prefer to choose their own partners. Economic realities of the time also account for small family sizes. In spite of the changes and influences, marriage, family, and kinship remain very strong, and some age-old traditions in gender roles are still practiced.

FAMILY AND KINSHIP

The family is a universal and sacred institution and the first unit of social relations. Usually formed by marriage, a family is the core of a household, and it exhibits intrinsic sociocultural values. Rwandans place high value on family and kinship as a means of continuing their culture and customs. Names, occupations, religions, and titles are marks of identity for families. Family ties are often a source of political, economic, and social empowerment in Africa. The Rwandan family is the center of activities as a social organization because it provides a forum for members to come together for recreational, religious, and social ceremonies. There are two types of families: the nuclear and the extended household.

In Western cultures, a husband and wife may constitute a nuclear family, but in African beliefs and practices children are the physical products of a marriage and complete the interpretation of family. The sizes of the families may differ because of the number of children, but without children a family is not considered complete. Because the husband or father is regarded as the head of the family and exercises certain powers, he controls many of the affairs of the family: economic, religious, and social. His responsibilities also include taking care of and protecting the household. Cooperation often exists within the family circle, but there is always distinction in gender roles.

A Rwandan family lived in a *u'rugo* (traditional homestead), which consisted of many beehive-shaped houses. A large fence enclosed many homesteads. The compounds were scattered on hillsides, and the houses were constructed with woven branches and grasses and covered with clay. Usually, the main family house was at the center of the compound. In contemporary times, these compounds still reflect the traditional patrilocal structure in the rural areas. Newly married couples usually prefer to live in a patrilocal residence with or near the family of the husband.

In African cultural practices, a man is permitted to marry more than one wife, and Rwandan culture is not an exception in this regard. In this situation, the household could include a man, two or more wives, and their children. Anthropologists believe that men who marry more than one wife are those who hold special economic, social, or ritual status because they need the women to assist them.[2] In the traditional Rwandan system, women were considered in an economic sense as producers. Hence, having more than one wife was a symbol of wealth and social status. In explaining why African men married more than one wife, Ester Boserup writes:

In a family system where wives are supposed to provide food for the family—or a large part of it—and to perform the usual domestic duties for the husband, a wife will naturally welcome one or more co-wives to share with them the burden of daily work.[3]

This shows that the polygynous marriage system in Africa had its foundations essentially in the economic activities of the people. Whether in a nuclear or extended family, there is a close-knit relationship with emphasis on respect for one another. Joking relationships also exist and involve one-on-one informal play and occur whenever and wherever members of two clans meet. It is an expression of humor in intergroup social relations.

SOCIALIZATION

The socialization process begins during infancy with the family playing a major role. In traditional Hutu families, the mother had a direct and pre-dominant interaction with the baby by nursing, washing, and watching over the infant during the day. Tutsi families were generally wealthy, however, which enabled them to hire maids to take care of the child as well as clean their homes. At night, babies slept in their parent's bed until the child was at least six months of age. The nursing, or breastfeeding, period usually lasted for the first year.

Tutsi children gathered together. Howard Sayer/Art Directors & Trip Photo Library.

Both parents constantly give instructions and guidance to the child, but the father becomes more involved in the child's life at the age of five. Aside from the father, the uncle contributes by overseeing the moral development and socialization of the child. He ensures that the child has proper education in Rwandan culture and customs. Social values and self-expression are encouraged, especially in storytelling. Home training at this time includes having the children participate in household work and vocational training in which they interact with their counterparts. As part of the traditional education, parents often put emphasis on home training and encourage their youth to become respectable members of their lineage and society. Among the children, acculturation and socialization take place partly by forming informal age groups. For boys, herding lessons and sessions of gathering firewood are conducted. Girls engage in lessons on cleaning, craft making, dancing, and singing. Socialization therefore helps the children not only become hard workers but also develop moral courage and emerge as meaningful members of the society. Rwanda, being a community-oriented society, fulfils the African practice of "it takes a village to raise a child."

Kinship has been a strong foundation of interpersonal and social relationships in African societies since prehistoric times. Kinship defined an individual's identity and served as a means of acculturation in addition to being an important source of economic, political, and social support and a safety net for members of the clan or lineage. Africans did not believe in individualism. They are predominately a family- and community-oriented society, and kinship formed into a basis of unity. Hence, whether in the patrilineal or matrilineal system of inheritance, an individual operates not in isolation but in a close relationship with other clan members. Rwanda has many clans, which foster close kinship relations. The royal clan was called Abanyiginya, and the clan of the queen mother was Ababanda.[4] Helen Codere states that "Clan had counted for something among the Tutsi and not the Hutu, and the royal road to office had been that of membership in the royal clan of the Abanyiginya or in one of the other clans of the high nobility."[5]

In Rwanda, a patriarchal system is practiced in which men exercise powerful powers over other members of the family and inheritance passes from father to son. Kinship groups are divided into three areas in Rwanda: the *inzu* (household), the *umuryango* (lineage), and the *ubwoko* (patriclan). In addition, there is the *ishanga* (a subclan of the Hutu) in the northern districts. The household serves as the core of kinship relations. An *inzu* consists of a husband, wife, and children (the nuclear family) in addition to close relatives (the extended family). The man maintains a strong influence as head and unifier of the family. The Hutu lineage is headed by the *umukungu*, the most influential male, who is rich but exercises little or no political power. The lineage consists of people from a number of households who have traced their descent to a common male ancestor. The *umukungu*'s functions include distributing land to lineage members, settling disputes, and representing the lineage in political matters. Among the Tutsi, there were powerful chiefs under the king who exercised sacred but absolute powers. Members of the patriclan do not have a strong kinship bond among themselves, have no chiefs, and have no social or collective activities that bring them together, but some of them perform rituals either at funerals or to ward off evil occurrences.[6]

CHILDBIRTH, NAMING, AND TRAINING

The birth of a child is often welcomed with joy and jubilation. Rwandan parents look forward to having a child, especially a boy to inherit the father's position and property. To Rwandans, children, especially girls, are sources of wealth because their parents will be given bride-price when they get married. Twins are often accorded special treatment, and rituals are performed to keep them alive. It is a common phenomenon in Africa for parents to have many children, thus making the families generally large. In the past, there were no established hospitals or maternity centers where women could give birth. Thus, children were born at home with the assistance of neighbors or local midwives. Shortly after birth, the baby is given a thorough bath with cold water, and magical lotion is applied to protect the child from evil forces.

For the first seven days after a baby is born, the mother and infant remain in the house, attended by family members. This is a period of seclusion, meant for resting and recovering for the mother. It is also a time of acclimatizing the baby to the new environment. During this period, relatives give presents to the parents and the baby. Fragile and helpless, the infant is susceptible to diseases and illnesses. Therefore, every precaution is made to ensure that the baby is in good hands. The baby sleeps in the same bed with the mother. Hence, Rwandans refer to the bed as *ikiriri* (big bed).[7]

As in many African societies such as the Yoruba, names are given to the baby on the eighth day. Names are important to the individual and family as a mark of identity and also reflect the people's cultural beliefs and practices. The naming ceremony is a special and elaborate social occasion for the family and the clan. In some societies, the clan or lineage head provides personal names for the baby. The names may reflect significant life experiences of the parents or the circumstances under which the baby was born. Names in African culture and customs always carry specific meanings.

In Rwanda, the naming ceremony takes place outdoors in the evening of the eighth day when family members and friends gather together to celebrate.

The process begins with the *gusohora umwana* (bringing the baby out into the public for the first time). The parents present the baby to those present for the naming ceremony. Because the mother and the baby have been in seclusion, this is the first time the baby appears in public. Although the naming ceremony is a social event, it also provides the opportunity for family reunions. Alexandre Kimenyi describes the process:

> Food and drinks are prepared by relatives and all the village children from three to ten years old are invited to the naming ceremonies. They are given a piece of land to cultivate. They use sticks that have the shape of a hoe. After a few minutes a male adult stops the farming activities by throwing water to them. They immediately run home because it is supposed to be raining. When they get home they eat while the adults are watching them. This eating is called *kurya ubunnyano*. When they have finished, they are each asked to give two names to the baby. All this is only ceremonial since none of these names is considered in the final name choice. After everybody has left, the mother gives names to the baby also, but as in the case of children, her names are not official either. The father is the last one to give the names. He can do it just after the mother has finished, or he can wait for the early next morning to name the child. There are no family names.[8]

Children undergo many types of training. For example, learning to greet and to respect elders is part of the early education. Training also includes how

Elderly Rwandan woman standing with children outside of a mud hut. Howard Sayer/Art Directors & Trip Photo Library.

to count, how to farm, how to tend the cattle, and how to relate with family members and neighbors. Parents provide examples because, according to a Rwandan proverb, "a he-sheep behaves like his father."[9] In other words, children imitate their elders or superiors. It is the responsibility of the parents to correct the children when they make mistakes because, according to an African proverb, "a tree is straightened while it is still young." Early corrections prevent a repetition of the mistakes.

LINEAGE

The lineage is a unilineal descent group of people who trace their ancestry to a single common ancestor. In Rwanda, lineage members form kinship units and reside in compounds known as kraals, with the oldest member serving as the head. A close-knit family relationship exists, and the members respect one another. Living together as lineage, clan and family members provide the strong support structure needed for economic, political, and social reasons. Lineage members also provide a support system in times of sickness, death, or misfortune. The ability to share joy and tragedy makes the traditional family and lineage system the bedrock of Rwandan culture.

BLOOD BROTHERHOOD

Blood brotherhood was a cultural practice that formerly was widespread in East Africa. This ritual involved two or more people who exchanged and drank each other's blood to validate their mutual faithfulness toward each other and their promise of secrecy. Secret societies often use blood exchanges to demonstrate their loyalty. In Rwanda, blood brotherhood was not a secret society but a secret pact of friendship that should never be betrayed. Blood brotherhood cut across ethnic lines: Tutsi men often took Hutu blood brothers, but neither the Tutsi nor the Hutu took Twa as blood brothers. Blood brotherhood was also often kept secret in order to prevent complication in judicial matters. If blood brotherhood was successful in judicial and social matters, it has been ineffective in preventing conflicts between the Hutu and Tutsi. Strong family and intergroup relationships are still maintained, but the practice of exchanging blood has been discontinued presumably because of modernization and the widespread cases of HIV/AIDS.

MARRIAGE

Marriage is a social institution that is accorded much respect and dignity in Rwanda. People desire to establish a family by getting married, raising children, and establishing kinship systems. In African culture and customs, being single, especially among women, is considered strange and unacceptable. An Ethiopian proverb states, "A woman without man is like a field without seed." Africans believe that marriage is not merely the union of a man and a woman as husband and wife but is additionally based on the relations between the two families or clans involved. Bringing the two families together is believed to further strengthen the relationship between the two married individuals as well as provide support and reduce the rate of divorce.

Marriage within each of the ethnic groups in Rwanda was common, but intermarriage between the Hutu and Tutsi has increased. Intermarriage is, however, discouraged in northern Rwanda. Because ethnicity was a consideration in one's social status, more Tutsi males marry Hutu women than Hutu males marry Tutsi women. When a Hutu man married a Tutsi woman, his social status was raised. The intermingling that has taken place in Rwanda leaves the determination of status fluid and flexible. Because ethnicity was a primary factor in determining where the children belong, the offspring of Tutsi women and Hutu men were considered Hutu. In Rwandan culture, bearing children out of wedlock carries the death penalty or banishment from the society. Illegitimacy remains a strong stigma to the woman as well as to her family.

BRIDEWEALTH

Like in other African societies, a Rwandan man pays the bridewealth to the family of the woman. The bridewealth is the money and/or a cow that the man's family pays to the woman's family in the process of marriage. Paid before the solemnization of the marriage, the bridewealth carried the purpose of validating and legitimizing the relationship between a man and a woman. It also was a control mechanism to stabilize the marriage. Bridewealth was part of the traditional social structure and marriage ethos that enabled the two families or clans to engage in exchanges of gifts in order to strengthen their own relationship. This shows that Rwandan marriage culture creates strong and reciprocal social relations not only between the two people being married but also between their families and clans.[10] Further, the rule of exogamy applied, which meant that the woman had to come from a clan different from her husband's.

Rwandans give great respect to the practice of bridewealth, irrespective of the form of marriage. In cases of divorce, the bridewealth is usually returned. Men often delay marriage because of a lack of money to pay the bride-price and/or a shortage of land to set up a new household.

PROCEDURES AND CEREMONIES

After the preliminary search for a woman and if the families of the two parties approve of the relationship, a period of courtship begins and culminates in a marriage under traditional laws and customs. The procedure consists of a set of rituals that will end in the transfer of a cow or other property from the husband's family to the bride's family. The preparation for marriage takes some time in order to allow the prospective bride and groom to know each other better. It is common in either traditional or Christian marriages for the families and the couple to have prayer sessions or consultations with the gods and goddesses before the marriage is consummated. The purpose is to ensure that the man and the woman are meant to be together. For Christians, the man should marry when he feels his partner is "bone of my bone and flesh of my flesh."[11]

In Rwandan culture and custom, marriage ceremonies are held at the residence of the groom's father, with the bride and groom beautifully dressed in traditional outfits. Family members and friends gather to witness the joyous occasion. The Rwandans have a system of traditional marriage similar to that of Nigerians, which was described by Toyin Falola: "During the ceremony, the family of the bridegroom will make statements of affection and promise to take care of the bride and her children and to meet all expected responsibilities to their new in-laws."[12] The bride is formally introduced to the family of the groom amid exchanges of friendly and joyous remarks. Prayers are again offered for the new couple by the parents of the two parties. Because the marriage ceremony is a social occasion, part of the procedure is for the family of the groom to provide food and drinks for the people. Dances are normally performed at marriage ceremonies because dance plays an important role in all Rwandan public activities.

MARRIAGE FORMS

Different forms of marriages are recognized in Rwanda. These include traditional or customary marriages, religious marriages, common-law marriages, and marriages through local authorities. In the traditional or customary marriage, parents and family members play a huge role in assisting their daughter or son in selecting a marital partner or in giving approval to the relationship. In some cases, parents prearrange the marriage partner or offer their daughters for early marriages. The involvement of parents and relatives emanated from their willingness to provide security and peaceful homes for their children. Africans often carry out a background check on the family of the prospective bride or groom before establishing contacts. For example, parents may oppose their child marrying into a particular family for medical reasons or to avoid bad luck. Individuals from the Hutu Abagesera and Abacyaba clans do not intermarry. Many such prearranged marriages have been successful, but in modern times, young people have started to move away from tradition by selecting their own partners.

Polygynous marriage is allowed by the culture, not only in Rwanda but generally in tropical Africa. By tradition, a man could marry more than one wife if he had the economic resources to maintain them. The family is the first unit of labor in Africa. Hence, the wives and children work together to maintain the family. Usually, Tutsi polygynous homes have two wives, whereas the Hutu have either three or four. In view of frequent rivalries and disputes, in a polygamous family each wife with her children occupies her own *u'rugo*. It is the responsibility of the wives to perform domestic duties such as providing food and beer for the household and cleaning their huts. Although the husband is the head of the household, overall authority is in the hands of his father and the lineage heads.

Procreation is an important reason for marriage; therefore, childlessness would be an excuse for a man to take more wives who would be able to bear children. Polygyny was encouraged by the practice of levirate marriage, whereby the widow of a deceased husband would be married to her deceased husband's brother. If the woman was still able to bear children with her husband's brother, the children belonged to the deceased.

Forced marriage, bride kidnapping, or marriage by abduction was practiced in many traditional cultures in sub-Saharan Africa, including Rwanda. It is not considered a valid form of marriage because the woman does not give her consent. This type of marriage often occurred among the young.

Christianity, colonization, and Western civilization introduced monogamous marriage. In Christianity, marriage is considered to be a lifelong commitment, with love, respect, and honesty between two individuals possible only through a monogamous marriage. During the colonial period, the Belgians promoted monogamy, and since independence the constitutions of Rwanda also have made provisions that impose it. Because monogamy is not an integral part of the Rwandan culture, it will take some time and drastic measures for it to be fully adopted by the people. Modernization and economic hardship are, however, strengthening monogamy and weakening polygamy among city dwellers and educated people. In the aftermath of the 1994 genocide, polygyny has reared its head as a result of demographic imbalances. Polygyny had become illegal in Rwanda, but some people see it as a practical approach to solving the marriage problems of the widows who have lost their husbands and younger women who are eligible for marriage. Against this argument is the increasing rate of HIV and AIDS cases, which is

prompting the church, government, and world health organizations to inten-
sify efforts in advocating fidelity and monogamy as against promiscuity and
polygyny. Although traditions are hard to kill, the high death rate may encourage many Rwandans to take to a monogamous form of marriage. In the
northern part of Rwanda, ghost marriages are practiced. This occurs when a
man dies before he is married. His surviving brother then marries a girl on his
deceased brother's behalf and names any children resulting from the marriage
after the deceased in order to give continuity to the deceased's name and his
lineage.

Rwandans regard marriage as a sacred institution, and they try to preserve
it. An elaborate procedure prevents divorce, but there is provision for it.
Parents and relatives often take part in conflict prevention and resolution
between a husband and his wife. If reconciliation attempts fail, divorce will
take place. A husband who initiates the termination of the marriage allows
the wife to return to her parents' house. When this happens, the wife's parents
must return the dowry to the husband.

GENDER ROLES

Precolonial African societies experienced gender inequality as a result of
their traditional cultural beliefs and practices. In male-dominated societies,
women were marginalized in economic, social, and political matters. Within
a household, men and women have different but specific roles. The differences are especially apparent in the type of responsibilities given and accessi-
bility to economic resources, such as land. In the culture and traditions of
Rwanda, women, unlike men, were restricted from controlling economic
resources. Women had no land rights because land was inherited on a patrilineal basis, from father to son, thus making women dependent upon men.
According to a study, "although land was held commonly by the lineage, each
male descendent was allocated a plot for constructing a house and fields for
cultivation. Forest and grazing land remained the common holding of the
lineage, and the lineage chief managed this common holding."[13]

Although women had limited rights to land and other economic resources,
they were engaged in agriculture, doing heavy labor to produce for their
household's consumption. Married women gained access to the land through
their husbands; they could use their husband's family's land. A Rwandan
proverb describes the position of women as, "A woman does not have an
identity, she takes her husband's," indicating the inequality in land and economic rights. At the death of the husband, a widow remained on the land,
holding it in trust for her male children. Even though women worked hard
on the land and produced, they did not have control over their income.

Women only controlled resources and surplus production if they could establish a one-to-one relationship with influential men. This reveals how Rwandan culture and customs have given men dominant power over women. Villia Jefremovas, in her discussion on the relationship of gender and class in Rwanda, asserted that "women, however wealthy or powerful, are restricted in ways that wealthy and powerful men are not."[14] During the reign of Rwabugiri (1865–1895), political and economic transformations took place. This reform eliminated the lineage system and replaced it with a clientage relationship. This arrangement favored Tutsi women, who became landowners, managers of land, and patrons like their male counterparts, whereas Hutu women could only sell their labor. A small elite group of Tutsi women not only could go to war but also could act as war chiefs, and they had the right to hold court sessions on behalf of their husbands.[15] Jefremovas also pointed out that "colonialism eroded the remaining institutions which gave women access to resources and intensified the development of institutions in which women's labour in household production subsidized men's labour in other sectors."[16] Women did most of the agricultural work, but hunting and warfare were, for the most part, exclusively masculine activities. Men engaged in hunting not only for game but also to protect their families from wild animals.

Many factors contribute to the transformation of gender relations in Rwanda. New laws have restored clan rights to land, but women still have limited access to land use in spite of their continued responsibility to provide for their household. The abolition of the feudal system placed all women (Hutu and Tutsi) at the same level in terms of their rights and production activities. In their different researches in Rwanda, Helen Codere and Villia Jefremovas assert that Rwandan women are now treated in the same way without reference to ethnicity.[17] Through the Ministry of Gender and Women Development, male and female children now have an equal right to inherit their parents' property.

TABOOS

Many things constituted taboos in Rwandan culture. Rwandans had several taboos about cattle, their owners, and their herders. For example, for a servant to receive a share of cattle, he was prohibited from walking behind his master or sitting on his stool. It also was not allowed for cattle to return to the kraal without fire being made for them. Again, in collecting fire for cattle, it was a taboo to carry only one piece of burning charcoal because one piece of fire was interpreted as a portent sign, which was an attempt to reduce the number of the cattle. It was wrong to smoke while milking the cow because they could die.[18] The taboos about cattle are indicative of how sacred the cows were among the Rwandans. In relation to warfare, it was forbidden for the royal drum to be captured by enemies because that meant defeat. Thus, the royal drum was often well protected, and whatever it took, the war must be won.

As in other African societies, talking about sex in the presence of children is taboo, and Rwandan cultural practices placed many linguistic restrictions on women. A wife was prohibited from calling her husband's brothers, sisters, or cousins by their first names. When a woman talked about her husband or members of his family, she was expected to be polite by using the plural form. Under no circumstances would a woman call her parents-in-law by name. This taboo is called *gutsinda* (when women are not allowed to name their husbands). This prohibition remained in place even if a woman was divorced. In the event that a woman inadvertently called her parents-in-law's names, she would have to go through a process of purification by drinking *isubyo,* a type of medicine that is administered by a traditional doctor. To a wife, her husband's uncle and his wife were considered her father and mother. Because of this linguistic taboo, a married woman was quite restricted in words when she addressed members of her husband's nuclear and extended family.[19]

Women were forbidden from whistling, presumably because they could not do it as well as a man. Women were excluded from building or fixing houses or compound fences. They were not allowed to milk cows and could not close or open the compound fence gate. It was illegal for women to cut firewood, and they were forbidden from tending cattle or taking the cattle to the well. If a woman was not married or did not have male children to do these activities for her, she would require the assistance of her neighbors. A Kinyarwanda proverb states, "Family businesses are affairs of husbands not wives." Essentially, these taboos support male domination and clearly make a woman dependent on a man. Since the genocide came to an end, women have become more assertive and some of the taboos are being gradually eliminated.

SOCIAL ORGANIZATION

The traditional Rwandan society was divided into complex but distinct social, ethnic, and occupational organizations. Factors that come to play in determining social status or social organization in a society include clans, lineages, wealth, and political power. In Rwanda, where several clans and three ethnic groups exist, Pancrace Twagiramutara argues that labeling the ethnic groups of Rwanda as Hutu, Tutsi, and Twa is simply "a system of classification, a series of onomastic emblems, banners or symbols serving to signal identity among members of heterogeneous social units."[20] If ethnic classification is inappropriate, the symbiotic division of labor may assist in understanding the distinct and hierarchical order in the social organization of Rwanda before and during the colonial period.

The emergence of the social structure was not a natural development but one created by economic and political power. By owning cattle, the Tutsi were the wealthiest and remained in the highest social status, whereas the Twa constituted the lowest economic group. With the establishment of the *ubuhake* system, whereby the Hutu (clients) served the Tutsi (patrons) political leaders, the perception and foundations of social stratification had been built. The possession of cattle became a symbol for social status, and the economic imbalance created a social gap between the three ethnic groups. A social distance was created between the Tutsi kings and their subjects, most especially because intermarriage with commoners was not allowed for many centuries. Thus, wealth and political power created a tradition of unequal social relations.

The sociopolitical organization of Rwanda that the Germans first encountered in 1907, under the leadership of the Tutsi, was suitable to their colonial administrative system. Controlling the people through the powerful Tutsi kings was to the administrative expediency of the Germans. In this respect, the Tutsi not only enjoyed continuing higher social status but also received support and more privileges from the Germans. Taking over from the Germans, the Belgians also allowed the Tutsi to exercise exclusive political and social powers.

The Tutsi enjoyed a privileged social standing through the *ubuhake* system. In view of the colonial support that the Tutsi aristocracy received, the Hutu were made to believe that they were lower in social status. Making ethnic or cultural identities a part of the ruling mechanisms was a direct invitation to volatile reactions. Thus, the ethos of *ubuhake* and that of colonialism not only coincided with but also deepened the social divide. This situation had far-reaching social implications on Rwandan society. The vestiges of this social organization before and during the colonial period lingered for many years after independence and were partly responsible for the genocide of 1994.

Although there was a symbiotic socioeconomic interaction, there was an apparent lack of social cohesion in early Rwandan society. This gave rise to the outbreak of several bloody conflicts. Admittedly, social interaction does not necessarily promote conflict, but when a group feels oppressed, violent clashes are not unlikely. The Hutu and Tutsi interacted socially, but the Hutu felt socially and politically deprived and oppressed. They reacted in what is generally referred to as a *social revolution,* which unfortunately culminated in the collective and coordinated violence of the genocide in 1994.

SOCIAL CHANGE

The social structure by ethnic affiliation that categorized the Rwandan society is no longer in place. Hence, the idea of the superiority and inferiority of the Tutsi and Hutu, respectively, has become obsolete. Intermarriage between the Hutu and Tutsi not only has fostered social interaction but also has helped demolish the superiority-inferiority syndrome. In modern Rwanda, people are identified no longer by their ethnic group but as citizens.

Gender roles also are changing. In traditional and modern Rwanda, the roles played by women have been crucial. In precolonial and colonial times, women were not in the forefront of politics, but today, women are actively participating in politics as senior officers. Western education is helping them make remarkable contributions to the growth of the society.

MODERNITY AND RWANDAN WOMEN

One of the major developments after the genocide is the development of new roles and opportunities for women. During the genocide, many men were killed, maimed, or forced into exile and unable to carry out their family responsibilities, and women emerged as heads of households. Instead of the man being "the central pole of the house," as a Ugandan proverb states, it is the woman who has become the pillar of the house in Rwanda. The female population has risen, and female-headed households have increased. A recent figure shows that women make up 54 percent of the population. Women head approximately 34 percent of Rwanda's households.[21] These figures prove that a change has occurred in gender and social relations in the aftermath of the genocide.

Women's responsibilities have expanded, and women have become increasingly active in all aspects of Rwandan life and culture. The traditional limitations placed on women and the unequal distribution of gender power no longer command respect in modern Rwanda. Moving away from the traditional system that restricted them, women are contributing significantly to strengthening the economy and promoting peace and unity. At the community level, women are forming associations and cooperative societies that empower them economically and politically. At the national level, the government created the Ministry of Gender and Women Development in 1999 in order to give women political empowerment and to mainstream gender into all its policies and programs.

Traditionally, women have been marginalized in terms of access to land, but the government has enacted new laws that support a woman's right to land and right to own private property. Although women still participate in agricultural production, basketry, pottery, and other economic enterprises, their conditions have profoundly improved, compared to the gender gap that existed in the past.

Rwandan women are increasing their involvement in political programs. At both local and national levels, women are advancing in political participation. To upset the gender inequality in politics, the 2003 constitution was amended to allow women to hold at least 30 percent of all positions in government. Through this gender quota, women have the opportunity to participate actively in decision-making at top government levels.

It should be noted that many aspects of the traditional culture, especially the taboos on women, are no longer applicable. The influence of Christianity, Westernization, modernization, and women's liberation are the reasons for the change. The change does not remove the cultural emphasis on politeness and respect, which are integral parts of African culture and customs. In modern times, a woman is able to address her parents-in-law as "the father or mother of so-and-so," using the name of the youngest child, or she can use the praise names of the individual. It is also possible for her to create a new name for her in-law, which will be understood and acceptable to everyone.[22]

Social institutions remain in existence and perform the functions of strengthening kinship relations and supporting one another, especially in rural areas. Rwandans are family-oriented and respect their social institutions. Marriage and kinship relations and practices, such as the naming ceremony, persist with some changes. Rwandans have not been influenced by individualism but remain connected to their kinship relations. The vestiges of Rwandan precolonial social organization did not immediately disappear either with colonialism or with independence. Due to the nature of the traditional social organization, in which the Tutsi monopolized power and status, the Hutu became displaced, and this engendered social conflicts. Making ethnic identities a part of the ruling mechanism did not foster social equality. Although continuous changes have been made in the social status of the Hutu and Tutsi, the Twa continue to be at the bottom of the social hierarchy. The previous means of measuring the social status of Rwandans by ethnicity or by the possession of cattle no longer exist. Instead, education, wealth, and political position have become the new indicators.

Gender roles also continue to change, but "Rwandan women still rely on their relationships with men to gain access to land for their own and their children's survival."[23] The number of female-headed household has increased significantly because of the genocide of 1994 in which many men were killed.

NOTES

1. Jennie E. Burnet and the Rwanda Initiative for Sustainable Development (RISD), "Culture, Practice and Law: Women's Access to Land in Rwanda," in *Women and Land in Africa: Culture, Religion and Realizing Women's Rights,* ed. L. Muthoni Wanyeki (London: Zed Books, 2003), 183.

2. Glenn E. King, *Traditional Cultures: A Survey of Nonwestern Experience and Achievement* (Prospect Heights, IL: Waveland Press, 2003), 12–13.

3. Ester Boserup, *Woman's Role in Economic Development* (London: George Allen and Unwin, 1970), 43.

4. Other clans include Ababanda, Ababega, Abacyaba, Abagesera, Abaha, Abahondogo, Abanyakarama, Abanyiginya, Abashambo, Abasinga, Abatsobe, Abazigaba, Abenengwe, and Abungura; Alexandre Kimenyi, *Kinyarwanda and Kirundi Names: A Semiolinguistic Analysis of Bantu Onomastics* (Lewiston, NY: Edwin Mellen Press, 1989), 14. Others include Abakomo, Abahindiro, Abatira, Abaniakaroma; Helen Codere, *The Biography of an African Society, Rwanda 1900–1960: Based on Forty-Eight Rwandan Autobiographies* (Tervuren, Belgium: Musée Royal de l'Afrique Centrale, Annals Sciences Humaines, no. 79, 1973), 16–17.

5. Codere, *The Biography of an African Society,* 30.

6. Marcel d'Hertefelt, "The Rwandan of Rwanda," in *Peoples of Africa,* ed., James L. Gibbs Jr. (New York: Holt, Rinehart, and Winston, 1965), 415.

7. Kimenyi, *Kinyarwanda and Kirundi Names,* 12.

8. Ibid., 13. This traditional naming system for humans has been adopted for the mountain gorillas. The occasion has become so elaborate and popularized that the Office of Rwanda Tourism and National Parks (ORTPN) invites international dignitaries to attend.

9 "African Proverbs, Stories, and Sayings—Weekly African Proverbs," http://www.afriprov.org/resources/dailyproverbs.htm.

10. Jim Freedman, *Nyabingi: The Social History of an African Divinity* (Tervuren, Belgium: Musée Royal de l'Afrique Centrale, Annales Sciences Humaines, no. 115, 1984), 84–85.

11. Holy Bible, Genesis 2:23.

12. Toyin Falola, *Culture and Customs of Nigeria* (Westport, CT: Greenwood Press, 2001), 122.

13. Burnet and RISD, "Culture, Practice and Law," 183.

14. Villia Jefremovas, "Loose Women, Virtuous Wives, and Timid Virgins: Gender and the Control of Resources in Rwanda," *Canadian Journal of African Studies* 25, no. 3 (1991): 379.

15. Codere, *The Biography of an African Society,* 246–47.

16. Jefremovas, "Loose Women, Virtuous Wives," 381–82.

17. Ibid. 392.

18. Peter Niyibizi, "Rwanda's Legacy," based on information from Aloys Bigirumwami, *Imihango n'Imigenzo n'Imiziririrzo mu Rwanda, The New Times,* August 11, 2006, 8.

19. This section on taboos is taken from Alexandre Kimenyi, "An Ethnolinguistic Analysis of Kinyarwanda Kinship Terms," Sixth Annual Meeting of the California Linguistic Association, Sacramento, California, 1978.

20. Pancrace Twagiramutara, "Archaeological and Anthropological Hypotheses Concerning the Origin of Ethnic Divisions in Sub-Saharan Africa," in *Conflict in the Archaeology of Living Traditions,* ed. R. Layton (London: Routledge, 1994), 94.

21. "Gender Assessment: Rwanda ISP: 2004–2008," Executive Summary, USAID Rwanda, February 27, 2003, http://rwanda.usaid.gov/images/Docs/Gender%20Assessment%202-2-03.pdf.

22. Kimenyi, *Kinyarwanda and Kirundi Names,* 106–8.

23. Burnet and RISD, "Culture, Practice and Law," 200.

7

Social Customs and Lifestyle

Cultural lessons abound in social cohesion and mutual understanding.
—Julius O. Adekunle, 2006

Socioeconomic differences in Rwanda did not drastically affect the common practices involved in some social customs, such as in religious festivals, the celebrations of special occasions, weddings, naming ceremonies, initiation rituals, sporting activities, and other forms of entertainment. Rwandans are community-oriented people, and they always have reasons for coming together. They also observe common holidays and, with a sense of national unity, celebrate Rwandan Independence Day, which tends to bring all the people together in a festive mood. In spite of modernity and Western influences, some aspects of Rwandan traditional customs remain, and people particularly in the rural areas have not been completely dispossessed of their customary lifestyle.

As mentioned in chapter 6, Rwandans developed close-knit relationships through which social activities and ceremonies were carried out. Friendliness, hospitality, politeness, and intermarriage serve as hallmarks of the people's lifestyle and social relations. Early European visitors to Rwanda, such as Count von Goetzen, the first German to arrive in 1894, who was later followed by other Christian missionaries (notably Catholic priests), enjoyed the hospitality of the Rwandan people. In the traditional educational system, children were taught proper socialization skills through learning about the appropriate ways to greet others, the importance of being obedient and respectful of one's elders, and being responsible individuals in the society. Where or when necessary, many children participated in ceremonies initiating them into adulthood or into religious cults. Through age-grade projects, activities such as dancing, drumming, or sporting competitions further served to promote teamwork among the children.

SOCIAL RELATIONS

Socialization, which begins at childhood, continues into adulthood when interpersonal relations become the pillar of the community lifestyle. Rwandan children are raised to observe and respect their culture and customs by participating in social activities. It is obligatory for children to greet their parents, and for wives to greet their husbands, each morning. Because Rwandans live in enclosures with many lineages, they could have many elders to greet. The elders also show their concern for the welfare of their children by asking questions relating to their children's in-laws, their jobs, and other similar types of questions. Keeping such close watch on one another strengthens social relationships. Children also are expected to do their daily chores before going either to school or to work.

Social relations promote cultural dynamism when people respect and understand one another. Good character or acceptable behavior is the hallmark of interpersonal and social relationships. In accordance with their culture, Rwandan youth greatly respect their elders and place high regard on seniority. Learning respect is a great part of the socialization and acculturation process for a child and is a part of home education. The culture does not permit the younger ones to look the older ones in the face, and a young person is not allowed to initiate a handshake with an elderly individual. The young look to the elders for instruction and guidance in social relations. Village elders and impeccable people *(inyangamugayo)* also give dignity to their culture by performing key roles in ensuring that people live in peace. They advise on or encourage good behavior and attempt to provide an example of a proper Rwandan social relationship and lifestyle.

An African saying states, "The words of elders are the words of wisdom." In the *gacaca* courts (the Rwandan cultural method of conflict resolution), the elders adjudicate minor cases such as claims to inheritance rights, land disputes, marital misunderstandings, and property damage, because the young are not considered to be capable of matching the wisdom of elders. No member of the society is regarded as a cast out because offenders are often quickly reintegrated into the community. A Rwandan proverb accentuates the centrality of the elders: *Ijambo ry-umukuru ritorwamo igufwa* (From the word of an elder is derived a bone).

In the preindependence period, kings were at the highest level of the social order. The position was sacrosanct and accorded an aura of dignity. Village chiefs and wealthy members of the society also received high respect. An unequal access to political power, a disproportionate distribution of resources through society, and ethnic differences, however, created social cleavages and animosity. In modern times, social activities have helped close the gap and solidify relations. The recent period of genocide disrupted traditionally legitimized institutions and was a betrayal of social relations. Nevertheless, Rwandans and the government are now attempting to deemphasize ethnicity, develop a unifying social system, and promote social cohesion.

The telephone is now part of the communication services that the government provides for its people. Formerly, the government was the primary user of the phone because the people did not have access to it. Kigali has become well connected to all the provincial capitals by telephone. Land lines and mobile phones are now available to support economic and social relations.

FESTIVALS

Religious Festivals and Initiations

The people of Rwanda have not completely detached themselves from the past. They embrace and keep their cultural practices in the many festivals and ceremonies in which they participate at different times and occasions during the year. One of their practices is the worship of ancestors, which was more common and more elaborately observed in the past than in the present. As part of their social custom, Rwandans perform rituals to demonstrate the interconnectedness between the living and the dead and to strengthen that relationship. These ceremonies are intended to demonstrate that the living do not forget the dead. Rituals are used to express gratitude for the favor the dead have bestowed on the living, and they accompany the bringing of requests to the gods or ancestors.

Given the diversity of African culture and customs, ritual performances vary when and in the manner they are performed from one society to another. For example, the ritual occasion could be religious, as in the case of initiation. The occasion could be political, as in the installation of a new king, or it could be social, as in the initiation into adulthood. Ritual performances also could include "initiation into new statuses, associations, or offices, funerals, marriages, other rites of passage, calendrical rites, healing rituals, masquerades, and other kinds of ritual occasions."[1]

Two secret societies that worship ancestral heroes (Nyabingi and Ryangombe) are known as Kubandwa sects, and their rituals called *guterekera* are performed during an annual festival. In performing the rituals, Hutu farmers often give tribute to Ryangombe, who was a mysterious ruler, presumably a

Hutu king.[2] During the ceremonies, the worshippers smear their bodies and faces with paint, decorate their huts, and undergo a process of purifying themselves by washing in a stream. A member of the sects carries a sacred spear, which is symbolic of spiritual power. Prophetesses participate in the festival, speaking a secret and esoteric language. The Ryangombe priests are responsible for preparing the sacred site for the rituals, usually a hut made of leaves. The priests wear dresses made of animal skin, and part of the rituals includes sharing of the traditional sorghum beer and the performance of ritual dances. Animals are killed and the blood presented to Ryangombe. On the one hand, the rituals represent the people's interaction with the spirit of Ryangombe and other ancestors, whereas on the other hand, they epitomize the protest of the Hutu peasantry against Tutsi authority.

The Festival of the Sacred Fire, with its complex rituals, symbolized the power that the *mwami* shared with Imana. Ritual specialists, the *abiru*, who were originally Hutu, performed the rituals, which were intended to bring good luck and prosperity to the agricultural and pastoral people of Rwanda.[3] The sacred fire also epitomizes continuity. Hence, every king renewed it in a secret ritual. The termination of the monarchical system brought an automatic end to this Sacred Fire festival.

Celebrated in April or May, Kamena (Taurus) is a religious festival observed by the whole community to commemorate the liberation of Rwanda from foreign invaders. Kamena was originally observed to celebrate the restoration of law and order, political stability, and economic prosperity. Hence, the Kamena festival represented a thanksgiving celebration in which subordinate chiefs and people from the provinces brought part of their plentiful harvest to the court of the king.[4] Kamena has been replaced by the celebration of Independence Day.

CEREMONIES

Many religious or social occasions call for celebration. Every culture supports ceremonies marking the birth of a baby, a wedding, or a funeral. In Africa, these, too, are traditional social occasions when family members and friends gather. The celebration can be on a small or large scale, depending on the wealth and status of the celebrants. In contemporary times, people celebrate their birthdays in an elaborate social manner, countries organize ceremonies to observe their Independence Day, and religious groups have different occasions for commemoration as well. All of these ceremonies in Africa are marked with food, drink, music, songs, and dances.

As mentioned in chapter 6, a common cultural practice in Africa is the naming ceremony of a newborn baby. The occasion is used to offer prayers for the baby's success, prosperity, and longevity. It also provides an opportunity for a social gathering of family members and friends. The baby is usually given a name that reveals his or her ethnic ancestry or the parents' religious affiliation. If the parents are Christians, church members are present to mark the occasion.

Marriage is one of the social institutions that the Rwandans consider sacred and necessary. All adult males and females are expected to get married because the society frowns upon being single. For women, marriage was even more important because it was a means of gaining access to land. The wedding process is a long one and involves family members and friends. Traditional music, songs, and dances are performed as part of the wedding festivities. In the nineteenth century, gifts during wedding ceremonies included baskets and milk in wooden bottles. It was believed that milk would bring good luck and blessings to the newlyweds. An important aspect of the wedding ceremony was the tradition of sharing a drink of milk or other beverage from the same container, using a long wooden ladle. Most aspects of the traditional marriage practices and procedures continue in modern Rwanda, except that in urban centers, marriage may now take place in the church, mosque, or government office.

Although death is not always welcomed, the passing of an elderly person is often celebrated. As the remains are buried, family members and friends remain silent in respect to the departed soul. A mourning period always follows in which a fire is lit for seven days.

INITIATION CEREMONIES

Many groups perform initiation ceremonies. For example, when the Kubandwa are inducting new members into the Nyabingi or Ryangombe cults, initiation ceremonies are performed. Both cults are considered secret societies, and each has its own special ritual procedures. Parents would initiate their children into the cults when they were experiencing some difficulties in their lives. The initiation ceremonies were performed in the open, usually around a tree with red flowers. The process of initiation to the Ryangombe cult, according Amiable Twagilimana, is as follows:

During the ceremony, previous graduates of Kubandwa served as role models for the initiates. Called cult fathers or cult mothers, they represented particular *imandwa,* whose behaviors and expressions were then imitated by the initiates. They taught the initiates the secret language used by graduates and songs honoring Ryangombe and other *imandwa.* The initiates were painted in white clay, acted wildly, and called each other by the name Ryangombe. They were also beaten and made to swear against their mothers. These behaviors were all part of the process of growing up and adopting the examples set by past heroes. Initiates regularly drank a bitter, red drink. This was a symbol of blood, suggesting that the initiates shared the same blood and were now all part of a new "family" consisting of all adults. At the final graduation ceremony, each initiate lay beside his or her cult mother or cult father for a few minutes, as if taking on their heroic qualities before entering a new life as an adult.[5]

Similarly, the Nyabingi initiation ceremonies are performed in the public. Nyabingi is a goddess of fertility, and the caves in Nyakishenyi (southwestern Uganda) are used as her worship centers. Worshippers can be initiated in the caves, and barren women who desire to have children can consult Nyabingi through a spirit medium. In promoting Christian beliefs and practices and in an attempt to discredit the Rwandan traditional religion, the European missionaries preached that the Holy Virgin Mary was greater and more powerful and better able to provide children than Nyabingi. This did not, however, stop the women from being initiated into the cult or from requesting children from Nyabingi.

The resentment from the German and Belgian colonial authorities and from the Christian missionaries increased the secrecy in the initiation ceremonies and practices of both the Nyabingi and Ryangombe cults. Christians were no longer permitted to participate in the activities and ceremonies of the cults. Colonial authorities opposed the Nyabingi cult because it served as a political movement, which did not embrace the Tutsi hegemony.

One of the rituals marking the coronation ceremonies of a new king was the reciting of the names of past rulers and their queen mothers. This is a long genealogical list of 43 reigns and three dynastic lines, which the Abacurabwenge ("Forgers of intelligence" or palace historians) must recite correctly. The list has passed from one generation to the next, and the practice was commonplace in Africa. The purpose was to encourage the new king to pursue policies that would promote peace, stability, and prosperity.

The celebration of the first fruits or bread feast, *umuganura*, usually takes place at the full moon in June or early July. Although *umuganura* was considered a royal ritual, its connection with culture and plants such as sorghum and millet indicates that nature constituted a central part of Rwandan religious beliefs and practices. David Newbury clearly shows that *umuganura* "was one of the major social and ritual events of the [Rwandan] kingdom, an annual festivity culminating at a time of plenty and rejoicing, and it touches on very broad questions pertaining to nature of society in general and the role of kingship within it."[6] For the ritual to be effective and the festival to be successful, the ritualists from the Swere lineage (Ega clan), robed in *nyarushara* regalia, must adhere strictly to specific items, complex procedures, and exact timing. Fire making was part of the process, and an anvil, baskets, hoes, and sorghum were the main objects of the ritual. During the festival, foreigners were prevented from entering Bumbogo, where the ritual was performed.[7] The ceremony was conducted amid drumming and singing.

The ritual remains important because farmers constitute a substantial proportion of the Rwandan population. The concept of *ubudehe* (working together) appears to bring about the communal celebration of the first harvest. Although individuals contribute the first fruits of their initial harvest, everyone shares in the food, drink, and milk. Collective sharing of the burden of work makes communal celebration of the harvest an enjoyable event. This emphasizes the point that Rwandan culture supports and promotes sharing and togetherness. During the ceremony, villagers assemble in an open place to share the first harvest of the year. Family members and friends share a meal and drink from the same bowl. Adults give milk, millet, and sorghum drink to children. To grace the occasion, girls in colorful dresses perform the traditional harvest dance. In addition, hoes, drums, millet, sorghum, Great Basket, and milk are used in the rituals. To bring the celebration to an end, the blood of a bull is smeared on the royal drums.

LIFESTYLE

In every oral culture, folklore preserves the history, customs, and traditions of the people. For many centuries, telling stories and folklore has been part of the oral literature and lifestyle of Rwandan society. An analysis of folklore can provide a framework for the understanding of the lifestyle or daily life of the people. Riddles, proverbs, and songs are integrated in the people's way of life.[8] Narrated mostly in Kinyarwanda or French, the stories are purported to teach moral, cultural, historical, and social lessons. Given the importance attached to storytelling and folklore in Rwanda, good storytellers are admired, honored, and respected because they help inspire the children to develop self-expression, communication skills, and oratory ability. Some stories such as the ones that glorified the Tutsi rulers and those that encourage ethnicity and hate are no longer narrated, however, because Rwandans are in search of a new way of life that will not emphasize ethnic affiliation. Storytelling and riddles are prohibited during daylight but are allowed in the evening. At such times, amusements can turn into storytelling competitions among young people.[9] Stories can span centuries, can range from topics on morality to education, and can run across cultures. For example, as in other parts of Africa, animals, especially tricksters (usually the hare or the tortoise), are featured in the tales.

NATIONAL HOLIDAYS

The Rwandan government has set apart some days as national holidays for either secular celebrations or religious occasions. These recognized national holidays are usually occasions for the citizens of the country to come together, setting apart their ethnic or political differences. January 1 is celebrated as a national holiday in many African states, but one of the secular national holidays in Rwanda is their Independence Day, July 1. On July 1, 1962, the Belgians granted independence to Rwanda. Following Independence Day is National Liberation Day, July 4, which celebrates the success of the Rwandan Patriotic Army in taking control of the country's political power in 1994 after the horrific experience of the genocide. Kamarampaka Day (September 25) marks the anniversary of the abolition of the monarchy and the establishment of democratic rule in 1962.

Secular Holidays

New Year's Day	January 1
Democracy Day	January 28
National Mourning Day	April 7
Labor Day	May 1
Independence Day	July 1
Liberation Day	July 4
Culture Day	September 8
Kamarampaka Day	September 2

Religious Holidays

Easter	March or April
Assumption Day	August 15
Eid al-Fitr	Depends on Muslim calendar (no fixed date)
All Saints' Day	November 1
Christmas Day	December 25

During religious holidays, Rwandans attend either church or mosque for special prayers and thereafter gather as family members to dine, wine, and enjoy togetherness. On Christmas Eve, it is common for children to go from house to house drumming and singing Christmas carols, receiving gifts of money. On Christmas Day, Christians go to their different churches, dressed well and in joyous mood for worship services that often are accompanied by dance, music, and the singing of Christmas carols. After that, family members and friends will enjoy delicious meals such as beans, peas, potatoes, and rice with beef, chicken, goat meat, or roasted steaks. Christmas and New Year are joyous occasions for the poor and are the only times they can afford to buy meat and prepare good dishes that they share with their friends and neighbors. People used to meet (in urban areas) and "dance the year out," as an expression of gratitude for living to see the end of one year and the beginning of another.

Children born and christened during Christmastime often receive special treatment. The concept of Santa Claus as a giver of Christmas presents is foreign to Rwandan culture, except for Rwandans who studied in France or Belgium where they have Père Noël (the French version of Santa Claus). The African version of Santa Claus is Father Christmas. The exchange of gifts at Christmastime is not common, but those who are able, especially people in cities who have been heavily influenced by the Western world and are able to afford it, do so. Unlike the U.S. experience, Christmas is not commercialized in Rwanda or in Africa in general. During the Easter celebration, Rwandan children also do not engage in egg hunting because the idea is not part of their cultural practice. It is, however, possible that children of returning refugees from English-speaking countries such as the United States, Britain, or Uganda or in churches that are led by foreigners practice egg hunting in Kigali or other main cities.

On secular holidays, prayers are offered in churches or mosques for the good of the country. Although the Christian festivals usually are celebrated on specific dates, the celebration of the Muslim Eid al-Fitr is not fixed. Unlike in other African countries, the celebration of the end of Ramadan (the month of fasting) by the Muslims has not yet gained the status of a national holiday because Islam is only just gaining ground in Rwanda. The holiday is determined by the lunar calendar. Eid al-Kabir, which commemorates the end of the pilgrimage to Mecca, is a two-day celebration. Muslims go to the mosque for prayers in new or at least good attire; they kill rams and make delicious food, which they share. Their Christian friends are often invited to celebrate with them. Children take the occasion to play with their friends in their compounds.

AMUSEMENT AND SPORTS

Rwandans participate in several amusement activities, most of which involve dancing and music. Many games and competitions are organized to entertain the general public, and people are always enthusiastic participants or observers. After the day's work on the farm or in the office, the evening is often spent in amusement and entertainment. In the traditional setting, evening activities include storytelling and riddles and jokes. Adults narrate stories that teach morals, history, geography, mathematics, or science. For the children, storytelling is not only entertaining but also forms creative thinking, self-expression, and the ability to make public presentations. The evening provides a relaxing and learning opportunity to the children. Children also avail themselves of the moonlight to engage in some pastime activities such as dancing, wrestling, skipping, reciting poetry, performing in plays, or simply playing hopscotch or hide and seek.

Rwandans are also fast runners, like their East African counterparts in Ethiopia, Kenya, and Uganda. In schools, competitions are held in track and field events, but usually only those who live near lakes or rivers are able to swim. In all sporting activities, there are no gender restrictions, thus both boys and girls participate and compete in a variety of sports.

A traditional board game that adults and children enjoy playing is called *igisoro*. Commonly played in Africa, *igisoro* is a carved wooden box with 32 holes arranged in four rows (8 holes in each row). The board is often fairly rectangular in shape, and the game is played with 64 seeds with 4 in each hole. The game requires two players, facing each other and taking turns. Each player picks the seeds from one of the holes on his side and distributes them in order to each of the holes. Players try to win the seeds on their opponent's holes, and the player who captures the most seeds wins the game. The game requires calculation and concentration on the part of both players. While playing, it is common for players to make jokes about each other, and spectators add more to the jokes to make the game interesting. There are three important outcomes from the game. First, sitting face-to-face is a sign of cultural interaction; second, the game requires calculation in order to outmaneuver the opponent, thus helping the children in their mathematical skills; and, third, the game promotes socialization.

Soccer (football) and basketball are the most popular sports, but in recent years, volleyball also has gained popularity. Fans follow three main soccer teams: Kiyovu Sportif, Rayon Sport, and the Rwandan Patriotic Army. Rwanda is producing young and talented soccer players. The national soccer team, the Amavubi Stars, has competed against many top African teams and has played against many European clubs. The Amahoro stadium is usually filled to capacity with fans who drum, sing, and dance to support their team each time the Amavubi Stars play a home game. Those not physically present at the stadium watch the games on television or listen to the commentaries (in Kinyawanda or French) on the radio. Rwanda participates in the African Cup of Nations soccer tournament that is held every year. For the most part, political and ethnic differences are put aside in support of the national team, and a win for the Amavubi Stars calls for an elaborate celebration in the streets, in public places, and in private homes. The performances of clubs such as the Rwanda Patriotic Army and the

Amavubi Stars clearly indicate that Rwanda is a soccer force to reckon with in East and Central Africa.

Other sports include chess, cricket, cycling, and tennis. Through the Ministry of Youth, Culture, and Sports, the government supports the sports because they provide vehicles that serve to unite and rebuild the country. Sports are seen as developmental tools and sources of empowerment, thus both male and female sports are encouraged. In elementary and high schools as well as in colleges and universities, teams are formed to compete against one another. Rwandans now talk about sports teams rather than of ethnic groups. The National University of Rwanda has male basketball and volleyball teams. At the Butare Youth Football Training Centre, young boys and girls are being trained in sports and to develop a sense of teamwork. Recreation for women includes adult female soccer clubs in cities such as Kigali. The Women without Borders initiative is to train girls in soccer as part of the reconciliation process.

CINEMA AND TELEVISION

The watching of cinema (movies) and television is a recent development in Rwanda. For many years after independence, cinema houses were nonexistent and television service was restricted to urban areas such as Kigali. The radio and newspapers also had limited circulation. Cinema provided an alternative to television in developing countries where television service was limited. In spite of the gradual expansion of television, not every Rwandan was able to purchase one before 1994, and during the genocide both radio and television became the instruments of ethnic and political propagandists on which messages of hate were broadcast.

Television is still in its infancy as a tool for entertainment and relaxation as well as an avenue for promoting Rwandan culture and customs. Rwanda Television broadcasts programs such as comedies, conferences, concerts, documentaries, news, pageants, and sports in Kinyawanda, French, and English. These programs are meant to educate and entertain the people. Rwanda Cinema Center was founded to encourage and empower the youth to develop as actors and actresses.

Television affords people the opportunity to watch a variety of educational and entertaining programs, such as soccer, drama, and concerts. Rwanda Television (TVR) has recently undergone a remarkable transformation by transmitting in different languages 24 hours a day.

FARMING, PASTORALISM, AND VILLAGES

Historically, a significant number of Rwandans lived in villages and rural areas where they practiced farming or pasturing. Environmental factors partly determined the occupation of the people, but the social structure played a major role in the classification of the Hutu as farmers and Tutsi as pastoralists. Because the Hutu have a larger population, there are more farmers (about 90% of the population) than pastoralists, but this does not mean that there was high food production. Hutu farmers were hindered from large-scale production because of small landholdings and the use of traditional labor-intensive methods and tools such as hoes, diggers, knives, machetes, and sickles. For the most part, these tools are still in use because farmers have not yet been exposed to modern mechanized agricultural methods, and the Rwandan economy has a weak base. For agricultural production, the family is the first unit of labor. Secondary sources of agricultural labor include seasonal migrant workers and cooperative systems.

Coffee is one of the cash crops produced in Rwanda. Although its success depends largely on world market prices, coffee production is contributing to the economic growth of Rwanda as well as helping improve the lives of its farmers. The government is using the cultivation of coffee as part of a practical economic and reconciliation program. According to a recent publication, "Coffee is being used in Rwanda to relaunch the economy as well as heal old wounds following the genocide. The Rwandan government is encouraging

Banana trees growing in the hills and countryside of Rwanda. Joan Batten/Art Directors & Trip Photo Library.

the creation of coffee plantations where people from both sides of the ethnic divide work together."[10]

Although the Tutsi were cattle owners, animal husbandry was practiced by both Tutsi and Hutu. Farming and keeping of livestock still constitute the main occupations of the larger Rwandan population, with each group competing for land. The changes that have occurred in social customs and lifestyle have rendered the classification of Hutu farmers and Tutsi cattle owners irrelevant because the new socioeconomic structure is no longer drawn along ethnic lines. Umutara, in northeastern Rwanda, is a cattle-raising region, where long-horned cattle are raised. In most of the rural areas, goats and cows roam the streets and stroll across fields and roads. It is worth noting that in spite of the economic changes and fast-growing interest in international trade, cattle raising still constitutes a central role in the Rwandan economy.

Traditional craftsmanship, which includes basketwork, carpentry, painting, silver work, and wood carving, remains as a small-scale business but promotes family values as well as teamwork. Rwandan women dominate the basket- and mat-weaving industry, and the men are engaged as blacksmiths and silversmiths, carvers, and carpenters. For generations up to the present time, craftsmanship has helped Rwandan families and individuals increase their incomes. Using a variety of timbers, specialized and skilled wood-carvers make beautiful figurines, small jars with lids, *igisoro* boards, and other works of decorative art. In addition, belts, handbags, hats, leather goods, and wallets are made with animal hides, and women produce various kinds of bead jewelry. Archaeologists and ethnologists have established the relationship between ethnicity and material culture through the traditional ceramic production. This is true of the Twa who are well known for their pottery. All aspects of craftsmanship prove the ingenuity and creative skills of Rwandans. Aside from tourists who buy them, many of the Rwandan works of art are sold in Western countries, including the United States.

Although cities are fast growing, villages and village lifestyles also are changing, though at a slower pace. The village dweller's poor economic situation and his sentimental attachment to a traditional lifestyle, combined with the lack of necessary social infrastructure, contribute to the slow pace of development in the villages. Farming, pasturing, and small-scale industrialization dominate the economic life of the rural regions. The people in the rural areas essentially produce the food and other products that city dwellers enjoy. To meet the basic needs of the people, the government provides amenities and services such as health clinics, roads, and schools (elementary and secondary).

AGENCIES OF CHANGE

The Rwandan society is not static, and the changes demonstrate the dynamism of the Rwandan culture. In some places and in certain aspects of the culture, changes have been minimal and slow, whereas in others they have been significant and rapid. Cultural changes have been dramatically influenced by many factors such as colonialism, Western education, modernization, and the genocide of 1994.

Colonialism has played a profound role in influencing the Rwandan culture. It is clear that European culture differs significantly from the African, and being in political control, the Germans and Belgians were able to influence traditional Rwandan culture. Colonial rule changed the political system, and through the introduction of Christianity, many aspects of the Rwandan social and religious belief systems have been altered from their original practices. For their political convenience, the Germans and Belgians changed some aspects of Rwandan traditional culture and customs instead of accepting and respecting them. Through time, Rwandans have come to accept and adopt many of these changes.

The introduction of a Western political system with its accompanying civil service, military, and police system eventually led to the end of the monarchical system. Rwanda now uses the presidential system. Western legal practices replaced the traditional judicial system. Although in contemporary Rwanda the *gacaca* (traditional courts) were resurrected following the genocide in an effort to try the numerous perpetrators, they remain a shadow of the precolonial system. In the traditional setting, members of the *gacaca* consisted of village assemblies to settle family or village matters. The judge, jury, and the accused were from the same village. After due process was administered by this traditional justice system, accused people who confessed and repented could gain their freedom. The judicial system was called *gacaca* (justice on the grass) because the participants often sat on the grass to perform their duty.

Western education has been a powerful transforming tool. The values and curriculum involved in the traditional educational system were remarkably different from those provided by Western educators, which was pioneered by Roman Catholic missionaries and later by the government. The aim of the Roman Catholic Church was to train priests and catechists. Hence, the curriculum of their educational system was essentially theology. The Roman Catholic missionaries did not have to compete with Islamic educators because Islam did not take any firm roots in Rwanda. They, however, struggled with Rwanda's rural population, which favored past practices over Western educational values and ideas.

Upon independence in 1962, educated Rwandans assumed the political leadership of the country, and since then Western education has emerged as a vehicle of modernization. Successive governments since independence emphasized primary education, underscored equal educational opportunities, and promoted educational reforms to meet the economic, political, and social needs of country.[11] Western education has influenced almost every facet of life in Rwanda: It enables access to employment, civil service jobs, political offices, and wealth or is simply a means of measuring social status. The emphasis formerly placed on elementary education has shifted to higher education, with a focus on science and technology. Kinyarwanda and French were languages of instruction, but now English is becoming widely used. The Editions Bakame, a publishing house, is promoting literature in Kinyarwanda among children with the objectives "to create and promote youth literature based on Rwandan culture, and instill a reading culture in children."[12] The idea is not only to encourage children to read in the language they understand but also to foster creative thinking, to be conversant with their indigenous culture, and know that their culture is as good as any other.

For many years, the traditional healing system has existed alongside Western medical care. In clinics, hospitals, and maternity centers built in towns and villages, Western medicines are used. Many people prefer to go to the medical centers for treatment, but others patronize traditional diviners. It is to be emphasized that Rwanda faces tough challenges in providing and improving its health services. More than before, the problem has become very apparent since the genocide. The poor economy and the huge population partly account for the inadequate care of survivors, especially children and women. In addition, the fast-growing number of cases of HIV/AIDS requires immediate and intense treatment. Given the fact that many Rwandans live below the poverty line, they depend largely on the government for medical care.

THE GENOCIDE AS AN AGENT OF CHANGE

The Rwandan society has learned great lessons from the genocide of 1994. Rwandans rethink their relationships and the havoc that the prominence given to ethnic differentiation has caused over the years. The genocide was unspeakable, but its aftermath is now yielding positive changes. The emphasis has shifted from ethnicity to integration and development. Although the healing process continues, the people are becoming more willing to live in peace and unity and deemphasize ethnic differences. They now experience more freedom than before.

Women especially are accepting and taking advantage of the cultural changes taking place in marriage, married life, and the control of economic resources. Ironically, the genocide was the main force behind some of the changes. For example, in the traditional setting, remaining single was frowned upon. After the genocide, when women outnumbered men because many men were massacred, being single gradually became an acceptable norm. Also, the socioeconomic role of women has been strengthened through access to land. Women are now taking a more active role in family matters, not only as providers but also in making profound decisions in household affairs. This is made possible because they are both the breadwinners and heads of households. Government authorities are providing more support for women who are victims of abuse, violence, and sexual harassment. In spite of these changing trends in favor of women, the cultural role of men cannot be undermined in the Rwandan society.

Learning from the past acts of violence, Rwandans are no longer focusing on the genocide but are thinking more about reconciliation, unity, and nation building. Ethnic divide had caused conflicts, hostilities, and violence, has caused untold human and material damage, and has considerably slowed progress. The rebuilding exercise, which is a slow process, involves Rwandans, world communities, and humanitarian and religious organizations.

Churches in Rwanda form partnerships with U.S. or European churches for material and spiritual support. Through their programs, churches are contributing to the social growth of the people. The new constitution of the country has deemphasized ethnic differences and outlawed incitement to ethnic hatred. Economic activities and cooperative initiatives with international organizations are helping Rwanda to refocus and reposition itself in a place in which there would be political, economic, and sociocultural transformation. From these various avenues, impressive social and developmental changes are taking place in Rwanda.

Shifting from the past bloody and violent ethnic and political experiences, the government of Rwanda changed its national symbols: the coat of arms, national flag, and anthem. Prominent in the coat of arms are the words *unity, work, and patriotism.* Included in the coat of arms are cultural symbols of unity such as a basket, a cog wheel, coffee, sorghum, two shields, and a sun.

The new flag, changed on October 25, 2001, has three unequal stripes of blue, light yellow, and green and a dark yellow sun in the upper right corner. The blue and green represent peace and hope for a better future, and the yellow sun is a symbol of a new dawn.[13] "Rwanda Nziza" (Beautiful Rwanda), with emphasis on the Rwandan beauty, culture, and the people's patriotism, replaced the former national anthem, "Rwanda Rwacu" (Our Rwanda) on January 1, 2002.

Many of the social customs and lifestyles of the people of Rwanda have been passed from generation to generation. Although some have continued, others have changed. The present has learned from the past, and in terms of social customs and lifestyle, the past has made the understanding of the present practices possible. For example, Rwandans continue to maintain close kinship relations, and the lifestyle of the rural dwellers remains almost the same in contemporary times. The impact of Christianity and Islam has been felt on religion, with the extinction of some of the traditional and religious rituals. Political changes have taken place because the apparatus of power shifted from the kings to a modern democratic and Western parliamentary system. The erstwhile political culture, social customs, and taboos that thrived in the precolonial and colonial periods no longer serve the interests of the people.

Social status and lifestyle in contemporary Rwanda are no longer measured by owning cattle or claiming royal ancestry but are measured by one's level of Western education, political position, the knowledge of and ability to speak French or English fluently, the building of good houses, and the ownership of material wealth such as televisions and vehicles. In the aftermath of the genocide, Rwandans created new social networks and new lifestyles prompted by external influences penetrating either from other parts of Africa or from the Western world. New social activities such as going to the movies and theaters and wearing Western-style clothes are taking place, especially among educated youth who follow social trend in other parts of the world. The social divide remains, however, between the rural and urban dwellers, and many social amenities are available only in the cities.

NOTES

1. Corinne A. Kratz, "Ritual Performance," in *African Folklore: An Encyclopedia,* ed. Philip M. Peek and Kwesi Yankah (New York: Routledge, 2004), 397–400.

2. The name is Bantu in origin and it means "Eater of an ox."

3. J. K. Rennie, "The Precolonial Kingdom of Rwanda: A Reinterpretation," *Transafrican Journal of History* 2, no. 2 (1972): 11–53.

4. The festival has four components: the ritual proper, the thanksgivings processions, the meal, and the exhibition.

5. Amiable Twagilimana, *Hutu and Tutsi* (New York: The Rosen, 1998), 34.

6. David Newbury, "What Role Has Kingship? An Analysis of the *Umuganura* Ritual of Rwanda," *Africa-Tervuren* 27 (1981): 91.

7. Ibid., 94.

8. Egara Kabaji, "Rwanda: Tales of Genocide," in *African Folklore: An Encyclopedia,* ed. Philip M. Peek and Kwesi Yankah (New York: Routledge, 2004), 401–2.

9. Ibid.

10. "Coffee: Key to Reconciling Rwandans," BBC World News, August 30, 2006, http://news.bbc.co.uk/2/hi/africa/5299286.stm.

11. For more information on education and reforms in Rwanda, see Susan J. Hoben, *School, Work, and Equity: Educational Reform in Rwanda* (Boston: African Research Studies, no. 16, Boston University, 1989).

12. Hellen Mwiholeze, "A Woman Fighting for Children's Literature in Kinyarwanda," *The New Times,* December 1–2, 2004, 9.

13. This is the third time the flag has changed. The first flag in 1959 had three colors—green, red, and yellow—and in 1962 at independence, a large *R* was included on the yellow line to differentiate Rwanda from the flags of other countries that had similar colors.

8

Music and Dance

It has often been said that everyone dances in Africa, and that Africa is the festival continent. In fact, an African proverb says that if you can talk, you can sing. And if you can walk, you can dance.

—Paul Kagame, 2004

Africans are very sociable people, and music has been a great source of happiness and inspiration to them. They express themselves in powerful lyrics, using proverbs and stories to support their music. Both past and contemporary events come into play in African music. Hence, history and culture can be gleaned through music. Most of the instruments are indigenous, but there are foreign ones due to Western influence. Rwanda is a country that clearly demonstrates the sociopolitical power of music. Not only did the kings enjoyed music, the commoners also were in love with music. Music has penetrated every facet of Rwandan life, and all the component ethnic groups produce it in different forms.

MUSIC

Music and dance are strongly connected, and their roles are immeasurable in political and social ceremonies as well as in religious festivals. An interwoven relationship exists between music, song, and dance, and they are all often associated with ceremonies associated with births, marriages, deaths, and festivals that mark harvests and hunting expeditions. Each social activity or event has its own style of music. Toyin Falola asserts that music serves as a medium of political and social articulation and helps maintain a social system of harmony and peace;[1] it therefore forms an important part of African daily life. According to Fred Warren and Lee Warren:

> For the African, music is not a luxury, but a part of the process of living itself. Although Africa is inhabited by people who represent many different life styles, the one common denominator for all Africans is their love of music and their almost total involvement with it. Music follows the African through his entire day from early in the morning till late at night, and through all the changes of his life, from the time he came into this world until after he has left it.[2]

For the Rwandans, music goes beyond being merely a vehicle of entertainment or relaxation and a conveyor of joy and peace; it also connects an individual to the spirit world. Music is a powerful tool that links different generations through entertaining performances.

Music features in epics that celebrate excellence and bravery, praise songs, and bow songs. Hence, music and dance constitute not only integral and important cultural and historical aspects of Rwandan life, but they also are part of the daily activities. Music is everywhere in Rwanda: heard in both the rural and urban areas and played in private and public places. Music could be spontaneous or organized. As gregarious people, Rwandans evolved a wide variety of music and dance that suited their cultural practices. Generally, Rwandan music is evocative and exciting, but its style and songs are divided along ethnic lines. For example, the Hutu have humorous lyrics about hunting and harvesting; the Tutsi enjoy epics that center on bravery, wars, conquests, and cattle; the Twa celebrate their hunting background.

Music and dance were means of relaxation. Rwandan rulers enjoyed musical performances and dances performed by the Twa in their palaces. Among the Twa, an adult male was expected to become proficient in music and dance. Music and dance were used for the continuity of tradition, as in the *intore* dance of the Tutsi, and to promote intercommunity relationships. Because the Rwandan people were sociable and humorous, they composed traditional songs that expressed their emotions as well as their love for one another.

For the people of Rwanda, music held their sociopolitical history. In the traditional ethnic division of labor, the Twa were hunters, musicians, and dancers. They often performed for the kings because music and performance art went hand in hand with the cultural practices and warrior tradition of the Tutsi. Although Rwandan music is essentially vocal, it is always accompanied by dances. Although men, especially the Tutsi, dance to demonstrate their bravery and power, women dance to express their love and care.

MUSICAL GENRES

There are variations in traditional Rwandan music, including instrumental, vocal, vocal-instrumental, and vocal-instrumental with dancing. Vocal music is associated with songs that relate to historical occurrences, royalty, heroes, and love. Pastoral songs, hunting songs, popular music, wrestlers' songs, or stories that teach moral lessons also belong to this vocal category. The combination of drums and various instruments without song is classified as instrumental music. Rwandan music also can be classified into three main categories: First, *indirimbo* are songs, which are meant only for listening and for enjoyment. They are vocal and produced mainly in the Kinyarwanda language. Second, *imbyino* are songs for dancing. The songs are rendered to allow a slow dancing pattern in which the dancer strikes the ground with his feet in accordance to the rhythm of the song. One form of *imbyino* attempts to educate about marriage in that it revolves around the life of a woman as a wife and her role in the family. Other forms of *imbyino* include the *intore* and *ikinimba* dances.

Third are the *ibitekerezo,* which are sung poetry or stories that are accompanied by an instrument.[3] Written in verses, the songs were learned by heart and transmitted in the original form. Hence, they form part of the fixed literature of Rwanda. These include praise songs, songs about cows, and dynastic poems *(ibisigo),*[4] with vast information on the warrior tradition of the Tutsi.

Ritual or sacred music was performed by the *abiru* for the king and for the protection of the people against evil spirits. It also was performed during ceremonies to celebrate courtship, marriage, and harvest. The abolition of the monarchy also eliminated the role of the *abiru* in producing sacred songs. Ritual music is still alive and performed, but Christian and Islamic types of music have become more popular. Rwanda, as a predominantly Christian country, allows the blending of some aspects of the indigenous music style into the church in order to gain converts.

ROYAL DRUMS AND DANCES

In Rwanda, drums carried importance beyond their sociocultural context. Because the Nyiginya clan founded the Tutsi dynasty, the *kalinga* (royal sacred drum) became its symbol of political power. Lesser royal drums, known as *ingabe,* surround the *kalinga.* Thus, royal drums have occupied a central political position. A Rwandan saying explicitly states, "He is king who has the drums." Again, to demonstrate the power of the king, it was often said that, "The drum is greater than the shout." The drum represents the king, whereas the shout refers to his subjects.[5] The shout of the people could not be louder than the voice of the drum.

The kings were sacrosanct and so, accordingly, were the royal drums. According to Amiable Twagilimana, the drums were "stored in a house where a sacred fire was kept burning. The drums were sprinkled with bull's blood to honor the drum and to enhance its power. The genitals of the enemies attached to the *kalinga,* which was therefore a symbol of Tutsi victory and superiority over other."[6] The drums were rarely brought out to the public; they were beaten only on special occasions, such as the celebration marking the beginning of the planting season to symbolize the rhythm of life. Royal drums were marks of identity and authority. Each ruler had royal drums, which were carried wherever the king went. In case of war, the royal drums were often jealously guarded to prevent their capture by enemies. The loss of the royal drums was tantamount to the loss of authority to rule. Jan Vansina emphasizes the importance of possessing the royal drums by providing the example of Ruganzu Ndori, the founder of the Nyiginya Kingdom, who defeated Kalinga and acquired his royal drum. Ndori of Nyiginya defeated King Cyamatare, "who lost his life, his dynastic drum, and therefore his kingdom."[7]

The king employed special royal drum makers and often performed religious rituals with drums through the *abiru* priests. Drummers play together in groups and in rhythms. When performing rituals, two dozen tall drums were placed around a central drum, and the drummers moved around the drums in a circle, each taking a turn to beat the central drum. The performance often included royal rhythms, praise songs, bow songs, and *abiru* drum rhythms. Hugh Tracey, who worked extensively on music in sub-Saharan Africa, identified seven royal rhythms.[8]

The Tutsi in particular composed epic and historical songs in praise of their kings. Many Tutsi were poets and warriors, and they focused their songs on bravery, military successes, and their ruler's accomplishments. In the royal circle, music was used to educate the younger ones about the heroic and historical past of the Tutsi. Royal praise poems were often accompanied by a genealogical list of the kings. King Yuhi III Mazimpaka (reigned 1642–1675) was described as "a remarkable poet-composer of inanga songs depicting the rise of the Tutsi kingdom and his own heroic deeds."[9]

Men and women performed royal dancing exclusively for the ruler's enjoyment. During the eighteenth century, King Mazimpaka introduced songs to the royal cows. Twa singers served as entertainers for the nobles and kings, "singing ribald, off-color songs."[10] Nyanza used to be the seat of power for the Tutsi rulers. Among the traditional materials in the palace were the sacred royal drums. In fact, the central figure of the coat of arms for King Kigeli V Ndahindurwa (reigned 1959–1961) was the royal drum. King Kigeli V even conferred the

Royal Order of the Drum on people within and outside Rwanda.[11] When the Republic of Rwanda was proclaimed in 1961, the centuries of monarchical rule came to an end, and the royal drums as well as the royal music ceased to exist.

Songs and poems were composed mostly by Hutu poets and ordinary Tutsi. Such songs or poems were often recited by the *umugaragu* (servant) to the *shebuja* (master). They were called court poems and attempted to not only praise but also entertain the king.

Musical Instruments

Rwandan music is essentially a vocal genre, so not many instruments are played. Instruments include drums, *inanga, ikembe, ingoma,* and *umuduri.* Most of the instruments are made and played by men. As mentioned previously, drums were associated with royalty but were also used in social activities and ceremonies. Drums served the purpose of making public announcements or inviting people to public meetings. Drummers carried the message of the king to the people using the talking drum. During the colonial period, drums were used in schools to signal their opening and closing and to mark special occasions.[12]

A Rwandan girl beats a drum as children perform a traditional dance. Howard Sayer/Art Directors & Trip Photo Library.

The *inanga,* an instrument particularly used in praise music of the kings, was believed to have been introduced by the Tutsi themselves but was played by the Hutu and Twa. Because of its royal connection, the instrument was seen as belonging to the upper classes. The *inanga* is a stringed instrument carved from a single piece of wood and played during rituals. It has a flat sound box (resonator) with concave sides and is about three feet long and 12 inches wide. Between six and eight strings are attached to the narrow ends of the soundboard. The sound box is often decorated with either star-shape or oval incisions. A single performer does both the playing of the instrument and the singing of songs that relate historical occurrences, personal experiences, or current events. Both men and women play this instrument.

Similar to the *inanga,* the *ikembe* is designed from a resonance case and a rectangular wooden sound box. Eleven or 12 iron lamella are fixed to the sound box and played with both thumbs. The instrument was introduced into southern Rwanda from the Congo in the early decades of the twentieth century. The *ikembe* is made by the Twa but played with other instruments by both the Twa and Hutu. Praise songs and themes that deal with personal experiences and historical events are sung to accompany the *ikembe.*

The *umuduri* is an acoustic single-stringed instrument made by the Twa but played by the Hutu. Like the *ikembe,* the instrument was introduced to Rwanda during the early part of the twentieth century. The string, made from plant fiber, animal gut, or metal wire, is tightly attached to a bow. A gourd is attached to the bow to serve as the sound box. The length of the bow and the size of the gourd determine the sound of the instrument. The *umuduri* is played at festivals or official ceremonies. It is played alone, without other accompanying instruments, and the range of songs that are sung to it can be about love, history, religion, politics, or social events.

The *ingoma,* commonly found in many parts of Central Africa, can be a drum or a dance, depending on the culture and language. For example, it is an instrument in Rwanda, but in southern Africa among the Zulu the *ingoma* is a dance, which boys and girls perform without drums but often accompanied by a chant.

With all musical instruments, players and poets need skill to pluck the strings as an accompaniment to their own songs. One musical instrument that has been introduced to Rwanda from other parts of Africa is the *ruharage.* Covered with goatskin on both sides, the *ruharage* is placed loosely under the left arm with a strap over the left shoulder. It has a short strap used as a grip for the left hand. Unlike other drums, the *ruharage* is played with only one stick, and it sometimes accompanies the *imbyino* (a girls' dance).

The Twa in particular play different types of horn flutes. Unlike other horn flutes made of bamboo, the *insengo* and the *urugunda* are covered with an animal skin. The origin of the flute is uncertain, but it was presumably brought to Rwanda from the eastern coast during the reign of King Yuhi IV Gahindiro (1795–1825), who established diplomatic and economic relations with various coastal rulers. A flute ensemble known as the *insengo,* popularized during the reign of Yuhi V Musinga (1896–1931), emerged consisting of five horn flutes and two drums.[13]

Various types of rattles accompany musical instruments and dances. For example, gourd rattles are used in the cult of the Ryangombe. Rattle bells are often attached to dogs while hunting. The *intore* and *imbyino* dancers always wear ankle rattles to add more to the sound of the music and to stress the rhythm of the dance. Along with the various musical instruments are three instrumental groups: the *ingoma* ensemble, consisting of seven to nine large drums; the *amakondera* ensemble of six to eight trumpets; and the *insengo* ensemble, consisting of five flutes. The ensembles traditionally played for the kings and followed the *intore* dancers.[14]

PERFORMING ARTS/MUSIC

Music and dance featured prominently in traditional ceremonies such as weddings, installations of kings and chiefs, puberty rites, and religious practices such as healing and ancestral worship. Although the Twa were musicians, the Tutsi were considered to be renowned dancers. Twa songs were composed to communicate their hunting and pottery culture. They use the *ihembe* (animal horn) and the *umuduri* (bow instrument) as musical instruments.

The *amatorero,* a dance performance by thousands of girls' troupes, is an impressive expression of Rwandan music and dance culture. The Tutsi *intore* dancers, accompanied by drummers, at times attempt to symbolize and often reenact the warrior tradition of the Tutsi. Alexis Kagame and J. Saverio Naigiziki have written about the *intore* dancers. Regional dances include the celebrated hoe dance of the north.

Aside from contemporary and secular music, religious inspirational, praise, and worship songs in French and Kinyarwanda also are commonplace. The proliferation of Christian ministries in the aftermath of the genocide allows the focus of Christian songs to be on unity and peace. The ethnic gap that has existed for centuries in Rwanda hopefully can be bridged through Christian music. In churches, organized festivals, and concerts, traditional Rwandan dances are performed along with Christian music and lyrics. Some traditional songs have been replaced by gospel-tinged lyrics. Rwandan Muslims also are producing music with Islamic lyrics geared toward reconciliation, peace, and unity. Additionally, modern instruments are used in the making of both Christian and Muslim music.

MUSIC AND NATURE

In Rwanda, and indeed in many parts of Africa, music and nature interconnect. Most traditional instruments are created out of the physical environment. The sound boxes, the gourds, the strings, and the flutes, to name a few, are made of either wood or animal skins. Drum makers possess knowledge of ecology and are familiar with the local flora. They are aware of which woods create certain sounds or pitches in particular types of drums or instruments. Similarly, songs are often composed about nature, using hills, rivers, trees, and animals as their subjects.

PANEGYRIC SONGS

Historical songs were commonplace in African traditional societies, mostly sung by elders and palace historians. The songs often required a vast knowledge of the people's traditions and reveal the history and values of the society. As happened in other African societies, the singing of historical and dynastic songs became part of Rwanda's social and political institutions from the inception of the dynasty.[15] It is believed that songs, as part of oral literature, are conveyors of culture and history; that is why drummers and singers are regarded as repositories of history. Tutsi royal poetry and songs help transmit the historical past of Rwanda.

Panegyric songs usually focused on the praises of past rulers, their recorded great accomplishments, and their failures. References to past rulers in genealogical sequence along with a description of their successful reigns were meant to encourage a new ruler to follow in the footsteps of his ancestors. Panegyric songs could be accompanied by music and string instruments or chanted by professional singers. Most of the panegyric singers were Hutu.

DANCE

Whether in the past or present, Africans have demonstrated their ability to dance. Although music is often accompanied by dance, not all forms of music or songs could be danced to. Dances can be organized or spontaneous. The type of occasion or the specific music determines the rhythm and the type of dance. Ordinary social and religious dances are distinct from warlike dances. Dance can take place in private or in public; it can be individual or collective. In Rwanda, all types of dances are collective; there is no solo dance, except when the best dancer does a solo performance in front of the group. Along with the wearing of costumes, dancers clap their hands rhythmically with the music as they perform.

Rwandan children perform a traditional dance in traditional costumes. Howard Sayer/Art Directors & Trip Photo Library.

Male and female dancers perform in separate groups and have their own form of dancing. Both men's and women's dances require physical fitness and mental alertness because they involve jumping, frequent body shaking, and sometimes violent movements. The movements beautifully synchronize to the beat and tempo of the drum or whatever instruments are being played. A strong interface and communication exist between the dancers and drummers and musicians.

TYPES OF DANCES

The *intore* is the best known traditional dance in Rwanda. Originally, the *intore* (the chosen ones) referred to the young men chosen to serve as military guards, but it became an intricate and technical warrior dance performed by combatants, accompanied by the *ingoma* drums. Warriors performed the dance to celebrate their war victories. The *intore* also characterized and perpetuated the Tutsi cultural identity. Jan Vansina expresses the importance of the *intore* for the continuity of the music and dance culture:

> From a cultural point of view the recruitment of *intore* from about ten years of age onward and their indoctrination in the ways of the court was to favor the unification and the development of the Rwandan language as well as the

refinement of its artistic expression, which was especially reflected in the practice of different poetic genres that were cultivated there.[16]

In the preindependence era, the *intore* was performed exclusively for the Tutsi kings, but today, in the wake of political changes, it is performed for tourists at the National Museum in Butare. The Intore Dance Troupe was established many centuries ago and continues to serve as a hallmark for Rwandan culture. The dance is performed by:

> Men wearing grass wigs and carrying spears. The background is a dance performed by returning warriors, celebrating victory in battle. The dancers move from side to side combining grace and complex choreography with a raw aggression. At certain stages the dancers stop, with arms outstretched and make blood-curdling battle cries. These calls are individual to each dancer and represent warriors declaiming the details of how many he had slain in battle. Battles traditionally involved Hutu, Tutsi and Twa fighting alongside each-other against a common enemy. The performance of Intore therefore has always consisted of warriors of all groups dancing together.[17]

It should not be understood that the *intore* is the only war dance in Rwanda. In northern Rwanda, particularly in Gisenyi, other war dances exist, such as the *inkaranka* and the *ikinyemera*. They are primarily Tutsi dances.

The *ikinimba,* danced by both young and single men and women, is performed as part of a courtship ritual. Songs that accompany this dance are focused on advising the future bride on how to deal with her prospective in-laws. Once a woman was married, she was no longer eligible to participate in the dance. The *ikinimba* dance shows the grace and beauty of Rwandan women as they emulate the movement of cattle with their arms.

The harvest dance is performed at the ceremony known as *umuganura,* which marks the sharing of the first fruits or harvest season. Because Rwanda was basically an agricultural society, the harvest festival occupied a central position in Rwandan cultural practices. To celebrate the occasion, villagers gathered in a public place and girls performed the harvest dance. Beating of drums and dancing accompanied the rituals of the festival. Dancers often wore colorful costumes to the admiration of their audience. The dance was an expression of gratitude to the god and goddess of fertility and to the ancestors who made a good harvest possible.

RITUAL MUSIC

Ritual music existed for both personal and public reasons. During initiation ceremonies, rites of passage, marriage, and funerals, ritual songs are rendered, sometimes accompanied with dance. Diviners use esoteric songs and chants in their divination practice. Ritual music was used to appease the gods and goddesses, to protect the people against evil spirits, or to avoid epidemics and disasters. In the court of the king, the *abiru* performed the ritual music. Ritual music also was a part of celebrations that marked hunting and harvest festivals.

Ritual dances include the *urwumana* (the unbroken circle), performed in an ensemble whose members are mainly Twa; the *touchi* dance, often performed with feathers; the *ikinimba,* a traditional courtship ritual dance; the hoe dance in the north; and the dances organized to celebrate and praise the long-horned cows. All of these dances must be performed within the framework of the particular ritual being celebrated, and the dancers are expected to avoid any deviation in their movements from the original version of the dance, because departure from the norm is not permitted.

CHRISTIAN MUSIC

As a country heavily dominated by Christianity, Christian music also is popular in Rwanda. Powerful songs are composed and rendered on Sundays during worship services or at prayer meetings and Bible study groups during the week. For Christians, music is a source of comfort, hope, and peace. It is an expression of love and connects the individual with the Supreme Being. Almost every musical instrument is used in Christian music, but people often clap their hands and engage in dancing. Songs are rendered in Kinyarwanda, French, or English.

In the face of suffering and tragedy, Christian music provides succor. Since the genocide, Christian music has focused more on love and reconciliation. Foreign Christian musicians go to Rwanda to perform in order to raise funds to assist needy Rwandans. Christian music is being sold on tapes, CDs, DVDs, and videos.

MODERN INFLUENCE ON MUSIC AND DANCE

Rwandan music and dance are a mixture of tradition and modern influences from other cultures, but the rich legacy of the past echoes in celebrations, festivals, and in the entertainment of tourists. Various Hutu dances are still performed on special occasions such as weddings, harvests, and hunting expeditions. Dances were performed in a kin group pattern. Along with births, weddings, and hunts, Tutsi dances also were associated with a warrior tradition. Semiprofessional dancers include the Intore Dancers from the Gitarama region.[18] The Intore Dancers perform for tourists through the

National Museum in Butare. Tourism has become an important source of revenue for the Rwanda government. Hence, the Ministry of Youth Culture supports paid dancers to perform traditional dances in public places on special occasions and for the tourists. The government is trying to promote dancing as a worthwhile and economically sustainable profession.

As part of their socialization process, girls informally come together in various age groups for cooperative works such as basket making. Working as a team, singing together, dancing together, and socializing together serve to fulfill the concept of living together. Indigenous education in the culture and customs of the society also is carried out in the age-group system. Girls learn and practice to perfect movements and steps in dancing in their age groups.

Rwanda has many popular musicians, bands, and dance organizations such as the female Imena Group dancers.[19] New stars are rising in Rwanda and are incorporating African (especially Congolese) and Western styles into their music. Some borrow the Caribbean reggae style as well.

Africans in general and Rwandans in particular are proud of their music and dance they treasure them so much that no ceremony takes place without a performance. Since precolonial times, music and dance have played an invaluable role in the cultural practices and customs of Rwanda and still serve as symbols of national identity. Music and dance continue to be integral parts of the civil, economic, and social life of the people. Today, much of the musical instruments and dance styles of the Twa constitute part of the national and public performance art. Although dances for the kings are no longer held, the *intore* dance is still performed, and it continues to express the beauty of Rwandan culture and to relive the warrior tradition. According to Jos Gansemans, "the *intore* dancers are now merely picturesque additions to celebrations."[20]

Rwandan children are taught the art of dancing, which accounts for why the dances have successfully passed from one generation to the next. Since the termination of the monarchy, music and dance at the royal palace has ceased, but the traditional dances continue to be performed, especially the *intore.* Indeed, as President Paul Kagame put it, Rwandans know how to talk, how to walk, and how to dance.

The beauty of Rwandan music is that it is dynamic in styles, lyrics, and performance, but some changes have been made primarily as a result of foreign influences. Indigenous traditional festivals are dwindling not only because of Westernization and modernization but also because they are being displaced by Christian and Islamic observances. Because of its dynamism, however, Rwandan traditional music is being modified to suit specific purposes. Although proliferation of Western music has not affected traditional dance styles and techniques, the music is changing, as reflected in modern instruments that accompany Rwandan melodies. Along with traditional musical instruments, professional Rwandan musicians now play accordions, guitars, harmonicas, and even have synthesizers. These instruments also are used in both religious and secular music.

In the postgenocide period, Rwandans are no longer singing and dancing to celebrate bravery but to reenact it on special occasions or for tourists. Rwandan music and dance are no longer used to promote ethnicity and conflict, but they are geared toward unity and sustainable peace. For example, the Inganzo Ballet, a group of teenagers drawn from three ethnic groups, has traveled to many parts of Europe to perform.[21] While the boys drum, the girls dance. The Samputu-Ingeli Dance Troupe, led by Jean-Paul Samputu, has performed in the United States to raise funds to promote unity and peaceful coexistence among the ethnic groups in Rwanda. It is worth noting that the Samputu-Ingeli Dance Troupe, as well as some other Rwandan troupes, includes members from the country's three ethnic groups. Tourists are always delighted when treated to Rwandan music and dance.

NOTES

1. Toyin Falola, *Culture and Customs of Nigeria* (Westport, CT: Greenwood Press, 2001), 162–64.

2. Fred Warren with Lee Warren, *The Music of Africa: An Introduction* (Englewood Cliffs, NJ: Prentice-Hall, 1970), 3.

3. Twagilimana, *Hutu and Tutsi,* 24.

4. *Ibisigo* is a collection of symbolic poetry that narrates the accomplishments of the kings of Rwanda in symbolic and glowing words.

5. The saying indicates that the king was greater than the people. In the affairs of the government, the people had no voice. Hence, the king, symbolized by the drum, exercised enormous powers over the people. Alison L. Des Forges, "'The Drum Is Greater than the Shout': The 1912 Rebellion in Northern Rwanda," in *Banditry, Rebellion and Social Protest in Africa,* ed. Donald Crummey (London: James Currey, 1986), 311–31.

6. Aimable Twagilimana, *Hutu and Tutsi* (New York: Rosen, 1998), 27.

7. Jan Vansina, *Antecedents to Modern Rwanda: The Nyiginya Kingdom* (Madison: University of Wisconsin Press, 2004), 44–48.

8. Hugh Tracey, "At the Court of the Mwami, Ruanda, Rwanda 1952: Tutsi, Hutu, Twa." CD, 1999, http://www.dandemutande.org/Catalog/cat=Music&artist=VariousArtistsHughTracey.

9. J. Gansemans, "Rwanda," in *The New Grove Dictionary of Music and Musicians,* ed. Stanley Sadie (Washington, DC: Macmillan, 1980), 355. See also Alexandre Kimenyi, *U Rwanda Rugari rwa Gasabo: Praise-Poems of Kings, National Heroes and Great Warriors of the Ancient Kingdom of Rwanda* (Sacramento, CA: Pan-Africa Publications, 1990).

10. Richard F. Nyrop, Lyle E. Brenneman, Roy V. Hibbs, Charlene A. James, Susan MacKnight, and Gordon C. McDonald, eds. *Rwanda: A Country Study* (Washington, DC: United States Government Printing Office, 1982), 102.

11. "The Royal House of Rwanda," His Majesty King Kigeli V, 2005, http://www.king-kigeli.com/monarchy.html.

12. Twagilimana, *Hutu and Tutsi,* 26.

13. Bamboo horn flutes include the *umurangi,* the *incuragane,* and the *ikanka.* Jos Gansemans, *Les instruments de musique du Rwanda* (Leuven, Belgium: Leuven University Press, 1988).

14. Gansemans, "Rwanda," 355.

15. Alexis Kagame, *La Poésie Dynastique au Rwanda* (Brussels, Belgium: Académie Royale des Sciences d'Outre-Mer, 1951).

16. Jan Vansina, *Antecedents to Modern Rwanda: The Nyinginya Kingdom* (Wisconsin: University of Wisconsin Press, 2004), 62.

17. "Inganzo Ballet," Carbizones, 2004, http://www.caribzones.com/balletiganzo.html.

18. Nyrop, *Rwanda: A Country Study,* 102–3.

19. Others include Nyampinga, Les 8 Anges, Les Fellows, Impala, Abamarungu, Los Compagnos de la Chanson, Bisa Ingenzi, and Isibo y'Ishakwe.

20. Gansemans, "Rwanda," 356.

21. Inganzo means "source of life" and derives from the mud that the Batwa used for pottery.

Appendix: Rwanda National Anthem and English Translation

Kinyarwanda

Rwanda nziza Gihugu cyacu
Wuje imisozi, ibiyaga n'ibirunga
Ngobyi iduhetse gahorane ishya.

Reka tukurate tukuvuge ibigwi
Wowe utubumbiye hamwe twese

Abanyarwanda uko watubyaye
Berwa, sugira, singizwa iteka.

Horana Imana murage mwiza

Ibyo tugukesha ntibishyikirwa
Umuco dusangiye uraturanga
Ururimi rwacu rukaduhuza
Ubwenge, umutima, amaboko yacu

Nibigukungahaze bikwiye
Uhore utera imbere.

Abakurambere b'intwari
Bitanze batizigama
Baraguhanga uvamo ubukombe
Utsinda ubukoroni na
mpatsibihugu

English

Rwanda, our beautiful and dear country
Adorned of hills, lakes, and volcanoes
Motherland, would be always filled of happiness
Us all your children: Abanyarwanda
Let us sing your brilliance and proclaim your high accomplishments.
You, maternal bosom of us all
Would be admired forever, prosperous and cover of praises.
Invaluable heritage, that God protects to you
You filled us priceless goods
Our common culture identifies us
Our single language unifies us
That our intelligence, our conscience, and our forces
Fill you with varied riches
For an unceasingly renewed development.
Our valorous ancestors
Gave themselves bodies and souls
As far as making you a big nation
You overcame the colonial-imperialistic yoke

Byayogoje Afurika yose	That has devastated Africa entirely
None uganje mu bwigenge	And has your joy of your sovereign independence
Tubukomeyeho ubuziraherezo.	Acquired that constantly we will defend.
Komeza imihigo Rwanda dukunda	Maintain the course, beloved Rwanda,
Duhagurukiye kukwitangira	Standing, we commit for you
Ngo amahoro asabe mu bagutuye	So that peace reigns countrywide
Wishyire wizane muri byose	That you are free of all hindrance
Urangwe n'ishyaka utere imbere	That your determination hires progress
Uhamye umubano n'amahanga yose	That you have excellent relations with all countries
Maze ijabo ryawe riguheijambo.	And that finally your pride is worth your esteem.

Source: Used with permission: www.nationalanthems.info.

Glossary

abachuzi. Traditional blacksmiths.

abacurabwenge. "Forgers of intelligence"; royal court historians.

abagirwa. Nyanbingi priests and priestesses.

abahinza. Hutu kings; "those who cause things to grow."

abanyabutaka. Landowners.

Abanyarwanda. The people of Rwanda.

Abanyiginya. One of the royal lineage of the *mwami.*

abapfumu. Diviners.

abasilimu. Elite or educated people.

abasizi. Poets.

abazimu. Spirits of the dead.

abiru. Royal ritualists.

agaseke. Small basket.

akazi. Work.

amakondera. Ensemble of six to eight trumpets.

amatorero. Dance performance.

Butare. A principal town that served as the educational and commercial center during the colonial period; formerly known as Astrida.

gacaca. Traditional court system.

gusohora umwana.   Bringing the baby out into the public for the first time.

guterekera.   Ancestor worship.

gutsinda.   Taboo for women not to name their husbands.

ibihunikwa.   Store away or put in the barn.

ibisigo.   A collection of royal poetry.

ibitekerezo.   Officially composed court histories; sung poetry.

ifuni.   Used hoe.

igisafuriya.   A goat and banana dish made in restaurants.

igisingo.   Royal headdress.

igisoro.   A traditional board game.

ihembe.   Animal horn.

ikanka.   A musical instrument made of bamboo.

ikembe.   Stringed instrument.

ikigage.   Alcoholic drink made out of dry sorghum.

ikigega.   A barn for storage.

ikilili.   Aeclusion for a woman who has just given birth to a baby. She stays in big bed while recovering from childbirth.

ikinimba.   Araditional dance.

ikinyemera.   A war dance.

ikiriri.   Big bed.

ikoro.   Tribute payment.

Imana.   Creator god, supreme being; chance.

imandwa.   Those initiated to Ryangombe.

imangu.   Tooden tool.

imbazo.   Scraper.

imbyino.   Songs for dancing.

imigani.   Proverbs or witty sayings.

imivumu.   Ficus tree.

inanga.   Stringed instrument.

incuragane.   A bamboo horn-flute.

indirimbo.   Songs.

infura.   Notables; first-born baby.

ingabe.   Lesser royal drums.

ingoma. Drum.

inkanda. Loincloth worn by married women.

inkangara. Lidded baskets.

inkaranka. A war dance.

insengo. Horn flute covered with an animal skin; a flute ensemble consisting of five horn flutes and two drums.

intara. Winnowing baskets.

interahamwe. "Those who attack together"; took a new meaning during the genocide.

intore. "The chosen ones"; royal court dancers.

inyangamugayo. Impeccable people.

inyenzi. Cockroaches; took a new meaning during the genocide.

inzu. Traditional hut or household.

ishabure. Cloth made of goat's skin.

ishanga. A subclan of the Hutu.

isombe. Cassava leaves.

isubyo. Medicine; magic potion.

isuka. Hoe.

kalinga. Sacred drum that was the *mwami*'s symbol of authority.

Kinyamateka. Name of a Kinyarwanda-language newspaper.

Kubandwa. An important religious complex, a cult.

kunywana. To seal friendship by way of blood.

matoke. Cooked banana or plantain.

mizuzu. Fried plantains.

mutwale wa buttaka. Chief of landholders.

mutwale wa ingabo. Chief of men responsible for recruiting soldiers for the king.

mutwale wa inka. Chief of the shepherds.

muzungu. A white person.

mwami. Sacred king.

Nyabingi. Venerated female spirit.

nyarushara. Priestly regalia won by the Swere priests.

ruharage. Drum.

rumanura. Famine.

Ryangombe.   The lord of the spirits.

shebuja.   Patron; master.

touchi.   Ritual dance often performed with feathers.

ubucurabwenge.   A royal genealogical list.

ubudehe.   A traditional Rwandan practice of collective work.

ubugali.   Cassava meal.

ubuhake.   Forced labor.

uburetwa.   Customary work.

ubutega.   Anklet or bracelet.

ubwiru.   Royal ritualists who performed complex religious rituals and served as religious and political advisors to the king; a set of royal rituals.

ubwoko.   Patriclan.

umuduri.   Bow instrument.

umuganda.   Collective labor.

umuganura.   The first fruits or bread feast.

umugaragu.   A servant.

umugaragu or *sabagaragu.*   Client.

umuhoro.   Machetes.

umukungu.   Somebody who has riches and is able to feed his family.

umunyamukenke.   Cattle chief.

umupfumu.   Witch doctor.

umurangi.   A bamboo horn-flute.

umurinzi.   A special tree.

umuryango.   A form of kinship unit; lineage.

umusozi.   Hill.

umutsima.   A dish of corn pasta.

umuzimu.   Spirit.

u'rugo.   A traditional Rwandan homestead.

urugunda.   Horn flute covered with an animal skin.

urwagwa.   A traditional banana beer.

urwumana.   "The unbroken circle"; ritual dance.

Bibliography

Several books on Rwanda have been published in Belgium in the French language, some are in Kinyarwanda, and a few are in English. I received help from people who speak French and Kinyarwanda. Numerous books have been published on the recent genocide, making references to the precolonial history and emphasizing ethnic division to justify their arguments or viewpoints. The books in this bibliography are the ones I have cited or consulted.

Barnett, Michael. *Eyewitness to a Genocide: The United Nations.* Ithaca, NY: Cornell University Press, 2002.

Adekunle, Julius O. *Politics and Society in Nigeria's Middle Belt: Borgu and the Emergence of a Political Identity.* Trenton, NJ: Africa World Press, 2004.

Bartov, Omer, and Phyllis Mack, eds. *In God's Name: Genocide and Religion in the Twentieth Century.* New York: Bedrghahn Books, 2001.

Berkley, Bill. *The Graves Are Not Yet Full.* New York: Basic Books, 2001.

Boserup, Ester. *Woman's Role in Economic Development.* London: George Allen and Unwin, 1970.

Braun, Joachim von, Hartwig De Haen, and Juergen Blanken. *Commercialization of Agriculture under Population Pressure: Effects on Production, Consumption, and Nutrition in Rwanda.* Washington, DC: International Food Policy Research Institute, Research Report 85, 1991.

Burnet, Jennie E., and the Rwanda Initiative for Sustainable Development (RISD). "Culture, Practice and Law: Women's Access to Land in Rwanda." In *Women and Land in Africa: Culture, Religion and Realizing Women's Rights,* ed. L. Muthoni Wanyeki. London: Zed Books, 2003.

Callaghy, Thomas M., and John Ravenhill, eds. *Hemmed In: Responses to Africa's Economic Decline*. New York: Columbia University Press, 1993.

Carr, Rosamond Halsey. *Land of a Thousand Hills: My Life in Rwanda*. New York: Viking/Allen Lane, 1999.

Chrétien, Jean-Pierre. *Rwanda: Les média du Génocide*. Paris: Editions Karthala, 1995.

Codere, H. *The Biography of an African Society, Rwanda 1900–1960: Based on Forty-Eight Rwandan Autobiographies*. Tervuren, Belgium: Musée Royal de l'Afrique Central, Annales Sciences Humaines, no. 79, 1973.

Coupez, A., and Th. Kamanzi. *Recits historiques Rwanda*. Tervuren, Belgium: Musée Royal de l'Afrique Central, 1962.

Des Forges, Alison L. "'The Drum Is Greater than the Shout': The 1912 Rebellion in Northern Rwanda." In *Banditry, Rebellion and Social Protest in Africa,* ed. Donald Crummey. London: James Currey, 1986.

Dugger, Celia W. "Overfarming African Land Is Worsening Hunger Crisis." *The New York Times,* March 31, 2006, A7.

Durr, G. *Potato Production and Utilization in Rwanda*. Lima, Peru: International Potato Center, 1983.

Eller, Jack David. *From Culture to Ethnicity to Conflict: An Anthropological Perspective on International Ethnic Conflict*. Ann Arbor: University of Michigan Press, 1999.

Falola, Toyin. *Culture and Customs of Nigeria*. Westport, CT: Greenwood Press, 2001.

Feil, Scott R. *Preventing Genocide: How the Early Use of Force Might Have Succeeded in Rwanda*. New York: Carnegie Corporation, 1998.

Freedman, Jim. *Nyabingi: The Social History of an African Divinity,* Tervuren, Belgium, Musée Royal de l'Afrique Centrale, Annales Sciences Humaines, no. 115, 1984.

Gansemans, J. "Rwanda." In *The New Grove Dictionary of Music and Musicians,* ed. Stanley Sadie. Washington, DC: Macmillan, 1980.

Gansemans, Jos. *Les instruments de musique du Rwanda*. Leuven, Belgium: Leuven University Press, 1988.

Gibbs, James L., Jr., ed. *Peoples of Africa*. New York: Holt, Rinehart and Winston, 1965.

Golde, Peggy. *Women in the Field: Anthropological Experiences*. 2nd ed. Berkeley and Los Angeles: University of California Press, 1986.

Gravel, Pierre Bettez. *Remera: A Community in Eastern Ruanda*. The Hague, Netherlands: Mouton, 1968.

Hertefelt, M. d', and A. Coupez. *La royauté sacrée de l'ancien Rwanda*. Tervuren, Belgium: Musée Royal de l'Afrique Centrale, Annales Sciences Humaines, no. 52, 1964.

Heusch, Luc de. *Le Rwanda et la civilization interlacustre*. Brussels, Belgium: Université libre de Bruxelles, Institut de Sociologie, 1966.

Hoben, Susan J. *School, Work, and Equity: Educational Reform in Rwanda*. Boston: African Research Studies, no. 16, Boston University, 1989.

Imvaho, Nshya. Rwanda newspaper in Kinyarwanda, Kigali, 2006.

Isichei, Elizabeth. *A History of Christianity in Africa.* Lawrenceville, NJ: Africa World Press, 1995.

Jefremovas, Villia. "Contested Identities: Power and the Fictions of Ethnicity, Ethnography and History in Rwanda." *Anthropologica* 39 (1997): 91–104.

———. "Loose Women, Virtuous Wives, and Timid Virgins: Gender and the Control of Resources in Rwanda." *Canadian Journal of African Studies* 25, no. 3 (1991), 378–395.

John S. Mbiti. *African Religions and Philosophy.* London: Heinemann, 1969.

Jouannet, Francis, ed. *Kinyarwanda, langue Bantu du Rwanda.* Paris: Société d'Études Linguistigues de France (SELAF), 1983.

Kabaji, Egara. "Rwanda: Tales of Genocide." In *African Folklore: An Encyclopedia,* ed. Philip M. Peek and Kwesi Yankah. New York: Routledge, 2004.

Kagame, Alexis. *La Poésie dynastique au Rwanda.* Brussels, Belgium: Académie Royale des Sciences d'Outre-Mer, 1951.

Kimenyi, Alexandre. "An Ethnolinguistic Analysis of Kinyarwanda Kinship Terms." Sixth Annual Meeting of the California Linguistic Association, Sacramento, California, 1978.

———. *Kinyarwanda and Kirundi Names: A Semiolinguistic Analysis of Bantu Onomastics.* Lewiston, NY: Edwin Mellen Press, 1989.

———. *A Relational Grammar of Kinyarwanda.* Berkeley and Los Angeles: University of California Press, 1980.

———. *A Tonal Grammar of Kinyarwanda.* Lewiston, NY: E. Mellen Press, 2002.

———. *U Rwanda Rugari rwa Gasabo: Ibyivugo By'abami N'intwari Z'u Rwanda* (Rwanda: The Genesis of a Nation). Sacramento, CA: Pan-Africa Publications, 1990. The book is divided into five sections, including praise poems, the genealogy of the kings of Rwanda, all the national military companies since the birth of the nation, the structure of the praise poems, and the poetic vocabulary.

———. *U Rwanda Rugari rwa Gasabo: Praise-Poems of Kings, National Heroes and Great Warriors of the Ancient Kingdom of Rwanda.* Sacramento, CA: Pan-Africa Publications, 1990.

King, Glenn E. *Traditional Cultures: A Survey of Nonwestern Experience and Achievement.* Prospect Heights, IL: Waveland Press, 2003.

Kratz, Corinne A. "Ritual Performance." In *African Folklore: An Encyclopedia,* ed. Philip M. Peek and Kwesi Yankah. New York: Routledge, 2004.

Lancaster, Pamela A., and D. G. Coursey. *Traditional Post-Harvest Technology of Perishable Tropical Staples.* Rome: Tropical Development and Research Institute, FAO Agricultural Services Bulletin no. 59, 1984.

Lemarchand, René. *Burundi: Ethnocide as Discourse and Practice.* New York: Woodrow Wilson Center Press, 1994.

———. "Power and Stratification in Rwanda: A Reconsideration." In *Peoples and Cultures of Africa,* ed. Elliot P. Skinner. New York: Natural History Press, 1973.

———. *Rwanda and Burundi.* New York: Praeger, 1970.

Lewis, Jerome, and Judy Knight. *The Twa of Rwanda.* Copenhagen, Denmark: World Rainforest Movement, International Work Group of Indigenous Affairs and Survival International (France), 1995.

Linden, Ian, and Jane Linden. *Church and Revolution in Rwanda.* New York: Manchester University Press, 1977.

Louis, Wm. Roger. *Ruanda-Urundi, 1884–1919.* Oxford: Clarendon Press, 1963.

Mackenzie, Lynn. *Non-Western Art: A Brief Guide.* 2nd ed. Upper Saddle River, NJ: Prentice Hall, 2001.

Mair, Lucy. *African Societies.* London: Cambridge University Press, 1974.

Maquet, Jacques J. *The Premise of Inequality in Rwanda: A Study of Political Relations in a Central African Kingdom.* London: Oxford University Press, 1961.

———. *Le système des relations sociales dans le Ruanda ancien.* Tervuren, Belgium: Musée Royal de l'Afrique Central, 1954.

Merriam, Alan P. *African Music in Perspective.* New York: Garland, 1982.

Mezu, Rose Ure, ed. *A History of African Women's Literature: Essays on Poetry, Gender, Religion, Feminism, Aesthetics, Politics, Moral Values, African Tradition and Diaspora.* Baltimore: Black Academy Press, 2004.

Morgan, Timothy C. "Healing Genocide: Ten Years after the Slaughter, Rwandans Begin to Mend Their Torn Nation with a Justice that Is Both Biblical and African." *Christianity Today,* April 2004, 76.

Mwiholeze, Hellen. "A Woman Fighting for Children's Literature in Kinyarwanda." *The New Times,* December 1–2, 2004, 9.

Neuffer, Elizabeth. *The Key to My Neighbor's House: Seeking Justice in Bosnia and Rwanda.* New York: Picador, 2001.

Newbury, C., and D. Newbury. "Bringing the Peasants Back In: Agrarian Themes in the Construction and Corrosion of Statist Historiography in Rwanda." *American Historical Review* 105, no. 3 (2000): 832–77.

Newbury, Catharine. "Ethnicity in Rwanda: The Case of Kinyaga." *Africa: Journal of the International African Institute* 48, no. 1 (1978): 17–29.

Newbury, David. "Lake Kivu Regional Trade in the Nineteenth Century." *Journal des Africanistes* 50, no. 2 (1980): 6–36.

———. "Precolonial Burundi and Rwanda: Local Loyalties, Regional Royalties." *International Journal of African Historical Studies* 34, no. 2 (2001): 255–314.

Newbury, David S. "The Clans of Rwanda: An Historical Hypothesis." *Africa: Journal of the International African Institute* 50, no. 4 (1980): 389–403.

Nketia, J. H. Kwabena. *The Music of Africa.* New York: W. W. Norton, 1974.

Nkulikiyinka, Jean-Baptiste. *Introduction to the Traditional Rwandan Dance.* Tervuren, Belgium: Musée Royal de l'Afrique Central, Yearly Social Sciences, no. 166, 2002.

Nyrop, Richard F., Lyle E. Brenneman, Roy V. Hibbs, Charlene A. James, Susan MacKnight, and Gordon McDonald, eds. *Rwanda: A Country Study.* Washington, DC: United States Government Printing Office, 1982.

Nzabatsinda, Anthere. "'Traduttore Traditore'? Alexis Kagame's Transposition of Kinyarwanda Poetry into French." *Journal of African Cultural Studies* 12, no. 2 (December 1999): 203–10.

Peterson, S. *Me against My Brother: A War in Somalia, Sudan, and Rwanda.* New York: Routledge, 2000.

Prunier, Gerald. *The Rwanda Crisis: History of a Genocide.* New York: Columbia University Press, 1995.

Rittner, Carol, John K. Roth, and Wendy Whitworth, eds. *Genocide in Rwanda: Complicity of the Churches?* St. Paul, MN: Paragon House, 2004.

Scherrer, Christian P. *Genocide and Crisis in Central Africa: Conflict Roots, Mass Violence, and Regional War.* Westport, CT: Praeger, 2002.

Sibomana, André. *Hope for Rwanda: Conversation with Laure Guilbert and Hervé Deguine.* London: Pluto Press, 1997.

Sutton, J.E.G. "East Africa before the Seventh Century." In *General History of Africa. Vol. 2: Ancient Civilizations of Africa,* ed. G. Mokhtar. Berkeley, CA: Heinemann Educational Books, UNESCO, 1981.

Tadjo, Véronique. *The Shadow of Imana: Travels in the Heart of Rwanda.* Trans. Véronique Wakerley. Johannesburg, South Africa: Heinemann, 2002.

Taylor, C. C. "Rwandans." In *Worldmark Encyclopedia of Cultures and Daily Life,* ed. Timothy L. Gall. Farmington Hills, MI: Thomson Gale Publishers, 1995.

Taylor, Christopher C. *Milk, Honey and Money: Changing Concepts in Rwandan Healing.* Washington, DC: Smithsonian Institution Press, 1992.

Taylor, Christopher C. *Sacrifice as Terror: The Rwandan Genocide of 1994.* Oxford: Berg, 1999.

Twagilimana, Amiable. *Hutu and Tutsi.* New York: Rosen, 1998.

Van Noten, F. L. "The Iron Age in the North and East." In *The Archaeology of Central Africa,* ed. F. L. Van Noten. Graz, Austria: Akademische Druck- und Verlagsanstalt, 1982.

Vansina, Jan. *Antecedents to Modern Rwanda: The Nyiginya Kingdom.* Madison: University of Wisconsin Press, 2004.

———. *L'évolution du royaume Rwanda des origins à 1900.* Brussels, Belgium: Académie Royal des Sciences d'Outre-Mer, 1962.

Virchow, Detlef, ed. *Efficient Conservation of Crop Genetic Diversity: Theoretical Approaches and Empirical Studies.* New York: Springer-Verlag Berlin Heidelberg, 2003.

Waller, David. *Rwanda: Which Way Now?* Oxford: U.K.: Oxfam Academic, 1993.

Wassing, Rene S. *African Art: Its Background and Traditions.* New York: Konecky and Konecky, 1968.

Webster, J. B., ed. *Chronology, Migration and Drought in Interlacustrine Africa.* New York: Africana, 1979.

Index

abahinza, 4–6
Abanyiginya, 5, 100; dynasty, 5
abasizi, 51
adornment, 91
Africa, 32–33, 38–43, 48, 63–65, 68, 73, 93
African art, 64; culture, 48, 63, 91, 98, 101, 104, 107, 109, 112, 117; literature, 47; peoples, 47; proverb, 81, 103, 133; sculpture, 66; societies, 31, 48, 91, 100–101, 104, 140
afterlife, 28–29
agriculture, 3, 11, 12, 56, 75, 87, 93, 107
Al-Aqsa Mosque, 39
alcohol, 8, 13, 85, 86, 88
Al-Fatah Mosque, 39
amakondera, 139
amatorero, 139
ancestors, 15–16, 27–32, 74, 117, 140, 142
APROMOSA (Association pour la Promotion Sociale de la Masse; Association for the Promotion of the Masses), 18
Arab merchants, 38
Arabs, 39, 79
archaeological excavations, 9, 11, 71
architecture, 63, 71, 73, 75, 77

art, 63, 65–67, 71–72, 77
artifacts, 6, 50, 67, 74, 75
Arusha Peace Accords, 19–20
Assumption Day, 41, 122

babana, 69, 74, 82, 83, 86, 89
Baha'i, 40
Bantu, 3, 4, 6, 11, 27, 70, 71
basketry, 11, 63, 65, 68–70, 72, 77, 112
baskets, 11, 54, 63–70, 72, 74, 119, 121
Batwa. *See* Twa
beer, 13, 29, 83, 85, 86, 88, 106; banana beer, 13, 83; sorghum beer, 86, 118
Belgium, 3, 9, 16–19, 34, 48
beverage. *See* beer
blood brotherhood, 103
blood relationships, 30, 54
bride-price, 15, 101, 104
bridewealth, 104
brotherhood, 30, 36, 40, 103
Buddhism, 40
Burundi, 1–2, 4, 19, 22, 56, 69
Butare, 33, 35, 55, 59, 66–67, 70, 74–77, 82, 92
Butare Memorial Center, 66
Butare Youth Football Training Centre, 125

Cassava, 13, 70, 82–84, 88, 94

Catholic Church, 8, 16, 32–39, 42–43, 57, 128; Catholic mission, 8, 33

Catholic missionaries, 32–34, 41, 128

cattle, 2–10, 12–13, 73, 82, 84, 87, 103, 108, 110, 112, 131, 134, 142; cattle chief, 5; cattle dung, 73; cattle herders, 3, 4; cattle kraals, 73; cattle, long-horned, 127; cattle owners, 4, 5, 74, 127; cattle, taboos about, 108, 109

CAURWA (Communaute des autochtones Rwandais), 11, 71, 79n15. *See also* Twa

ceremonies, 27, 84, 87–88, 92, 105, 115, 117, 118, 137; initiation, 64, 115, 119, 120, 142; marriage, 73, 105, 119; naming, 102, 115; religious, 85, 87; ritual, 91; social, 98, 133; traditional, 139

chief, 7, 16, 18, 101, 107, 108, 117, 139; lineage chief, 107; village chiefs, 117; war chiefs, 108

Christian Council of Rwanda, 37

Christianity, 8, 16, 27, 31, 32–40, 42–43, 48, 97, 106, 112, 128, 131, 143

Christmas, 41, 44, 72, 122, 123

civilizing mission, 48

clan, 4, 15, 16, 27, 31, 32, 41, 73, 97, 99, 100, 101, 104, 106, 108, 109, 120, 135

clientage, 7, 108

Clinton, Bill (U.S. President), 22

clothes, 14, 31, 33, 65–66, 69, 81, 84, 89–93, 131

Codere, Helen, 100, 108

coffee, 3, 11, 12, 86, 88, 126

colonial powers, 8, 18, 33, 34, 37

colonial rule, 3, 33, 39, 128

colonization, 5, 8, 14, 42, 65, 106

craftsmanship, 71, 127

cuisine, 81, 88

culture, 5–16, 27–40, 47–56, 59, 63, 67–68, 71–72, 75, 78, 81–82, 84–112, 116–18, 120–25, 127–31, 133, 138–44, 147

customs, 6, 8, 15, 27, 33, 38, 47–49, 52, 54, 59, 71, 78, 93, 97, 100, 101, 104, 105, 108, 112, 115–17, 121, 125, 127–31, 141, 144

Dallaire, Romeo (Lt. Gen.), 22

dances, 11, 105, 111–19, 133–44; dancers, 6, 50, 71, 92, 134, 139, 140, 141–44; dancing, 28, 92, 100, 116, 123–24, 135–36, 141–45

death, 8, 15, 18, 22, 27–31, 36, 53, 103, 104, 107, 119, 133

decolonization, 17

deforestation, 2, 3, 11, 67, 86

Democratic Republic of the Congo, 65

Destexhe, Alain, 21

Dialogue, 35, 57

divination, 13, 28, 31, 85, 92, 143

diviners, 28, 31, 87, 92, 129, 143

drama, 52–53, 125

drums, 55, 60, 65, 67, 91, 92, 121, 135–42; royal, 5, 135–37

Easter, 122, 123

economy, 3, 9–12, 55, 75, 77, 81, 84, 111, 126, 127, 129

Editions Bakame, 51, 129

education, 8–9, 16, 38, 39, 40, 56, 59, 71, 97, 100, 102, 112, 116, 121, 125; Catholic education, 36, 42; farming education, 71; traditional education, 8, 100, 115, 128, 144; Western education, 5, 8–9, 33–35, 48, 54, 59, 97, 111, 128, 129

Eid al-Adha, 40, 41

Eid al-Fitr, 40, 41, 123

English, 4, 9, 48, 51–54, 60, 125, 129, 131, 143; English-speaking, 123

ESAF (Enhanced Structural Adjustment Facility), 12

ethnic, 4–6, 20, 36, 37, 41, 59, 81, 103, 109–11, 117, 119, 122, 124, 125, 127, 134; ethnic classification, 16, 42, 110; ethnic conflicts, 9, 18, 23, 37, 49, 54, 87; ethnic groups, 15, 18, 20, 31, 33, 37, 104, 109, 110, 111, 125, 133, 145; ethnicity, 104, 108, 112, 117, 121, 127, 129, 145

European colonization, 5, 8

Evangelical churches, 38, 42, 43

family, 4, 12, 30, 54, 64, 74, 85, 97, 98, 101–6, 109, 112, 126, 130, 135;

extended family, 14, 74, 100, 109;
family members, 14, 15, 29, 49, 101,
103, 105, 118, 119, 121, 122
FAWERWA (Forum for African Women
Educationalists, Rwanda Chapter). *See*
women
feudal, 7, 10
folklore, 48, 121
folktales, 59
French, 3, 4, 9, 48, 51–56, 60, 89, 121,
123–25, 129, 131, 139, 143; French-
speaking, 52, 53

gacaca (traditional court), 23, 30, 38,
116, 128
gender roles, 97, 98, 107–8, 111, 112
genocide, 3–9, 12–18, 20–24, 35–43, 48,
53, 56, 58, 72–76, 85, 106, 110–12,
117, 122, 125–31, 139, 143, 145
Germany, 9, 19, 20
gift-giving, 87, 88
Gitera, Joseph, 18
Gihanga, 50
Gisenyi, 3, 6, 74, 75, 83, 86, 97, 142
goat skin, 65, 90
gorillas, 1, 2, 10, 67, 86
Gotzen, Count von, 16, 32
Gowing, Nik, 56
Great Basket, 121
Great Lakes, 1, 12, 56
Gunner, Liz, 52
Gushee, David, 37

Habyarimana, Juvenal, 19, 20,
22, 55
Halord, Reverend, 51
Hima, 4
Hinduism, 40
Hirth, Joseph Bishop, 32, 33
household, 11, 14, 15, 55, 71, 85, 88, 98,
100, 104, 106, 107, 111, 130
huts, 14, 29, 67, 73, 74, 75,
106, 118
Hutu, 4–6, 9–22, 55–58, 65,
82–85, 99–112, 138, 140, 142, 143;
blood brothers, 31, 103; dances, 143;
farmers, 4, 10, 117, 126, 127; kings,

118; lineages, 6, 7, 100; power, 57;
Social Revolution, 17, 18, 19, 36

Ibisigo, 49, 50, 52, 135, 145n4
Ideal Democratic Party (IDP), 41
identification cards, 42; identity cards, 16
ihembe, 139
ikembe, 137, 138
ikinimba, 135, 142, 143
ikinyemera, 142
Imandwa, 15, 30, 119
Imbyino, 135, 138, 139
IMF (International Monetary Fund), 12
inanga, 137–38
Indigenous religion, 41, 42, 29–32, 35, 120
Inganzo Ballet, 145
Ingoma, 137–39, 141
initiation, 30, 117; ceremonies, 64, 119–20,
142; rituals, 30, 115
inkaranka, 142
*insengo*138, 139
interahamwe, 22, 39
intore dance, 92, 93, 134, 135, 139,
141–42, 144
intore dancers, 50, 139, 143, 144
Intore Dance Troupe, 142
iron, 5, 9, 11, 71, 138; iron smelting, 11;
iron technology, 6, 70; iron tools, 6;
iron workers, 9, 11, 71
Iron Age, 66
Isichei, Elizabeth, 34, 35
Islam, 16, 27, 35, 38–40, 41, 123, 128,
131; Islamic, 40, 135, 139, 144; Islamic
holidays, 41
Islamic Party. *See* PDI

Jefremovas, Villia, 108
joking relationships, 99

Kabgayi, 36, 60
Kagame, Alexis, 35, 52–55, 60, 139
Kagame, Paul (President), 20, 43, 133, 144
Kalinga, 7, 135, 136
Kamena festival, 118
Kandt, Richard, 16
Kanguka, 57, 58
Kangura, 57, 58

Kanyaruanda (Gilhanga's son), 5
Karisimbi, 1
Kavaruganda, Joseph (president of the Supreme Court), 22
Kayibanda, Grégoire, 18, 19, 34, 36
Kiga, 4
Kigali, 3, 14, 16, 22, 35, 39, 55–56, 63, 66–67, 70–77, 83, 85–86, 92, 117, 123, 125
Kigeri IV (reigned 1860–1895), 6, 7, 39
Kigeri V, 17, 18
Kigeri Rwabugiri, 11
Kigeri's court, 8
Kigwa, 50
Kimenyi, Alexandre, 102, 114n19
King, Glenn, 65
Kingdom of Rwanda, 3, 32
Kingmakers, 7
kinship, 63, 97, 98–101, 104, 114n19; kinship relations, 14, 100, 112, 131; kinship unit, 14, 103
Kinyabwisha, 4
Kinyagans, 12
Kinyamateka, 18, 35, 36, 56–58
Kinyamulenge, 4
Kinyarwanda, 3, 5, 6, 33, 34, 48, 50–54, 56–57, 60, 109, 121, 129, 135, 139, 143
Kirundi, 4, 56
Kiswahili. See Swahili
Kubandwa, 15, 23, 30, 91, 117, 119

land, 1, 2, 7, 9–11, 14, 23, 28, 42, 85–87, 101–12, 116–19, 127, 130; landholders, 7, 126; land rights, 107, 108; land shortage, 15, 104
Lavigerie, Cardinal, 32, 33
Le Grand Seminaire, 9, 35
leopard, 16, 32, 65; leopard skin, 14, 31, 65, 91
Lineage, 6, 7, 14, 73, 97, 100, 101, 103, 106–9, 116, 120

Mackenzie, Lynn, 63
Maize, 3, 70, 82, 83
male domination, 100
marriage, 4, 10, 13, 15, 27, 29, 52, 69, 73, 85, 97, 98, 103–5; intermarriage, 5, 15, 39, 55, 104, 110, 111, 115; marriage

forms, 105–7; polygynous marriage, 97, 99, 106
Mazimpaka, Yuhi III, King, 72, 136
Mbonyumutara, Dominique, 17
media, 55–59
metalwork, 11, 63
military, 5, 7, 10, 16, 18, 19, 32, 37, 41, 55, 128, 136, 141
milk, 10, 11, 13, 28, 29, 69, 82, 84–85, 88, 109, 119, 121
milking, 10, 108
missionaries, 8, 13, 16, 32, 33–36, 39, 41, 48, 51, 54, 75, 82, 115, 120, 128
monarchy, 7, 17, 18, 41, 122, 135, 144; monarchical system, 7, 36, 118, 128
Mpungwe, Ami (Tanzanian Ambassador), 19
Mukarugira, J., 51
Musinga, Yuhi, King, 33, 34, 139
Muslims, 21, 39, 40, 45n23, 123, 139; Muslim leaders, 38, 40
Mutara II (reigned 1830–1869), 6
Mutara III (died 1959), 17, 18
Mwami, 5, 6, 7, 9, 16, 28, 33, 35, 51, 88, 118
Mwiniyi, Ali Hassan (President of Tanzania), 19

Naigiziki, Saverio J., 55, 139
nationalist movements, 17, 18
National Museum of Rwanda, 59, 70, 74, 78n10, 92, 142, 144
National University of Rwanda (NUR), 9, 53, 58, 125
Ndahindurwa, Kigeli V, King, 136
Ndori, Ruganzu, 136
Ndorwa Kingdom, 73
Newbury, David, 120
newspapers, 4, 56–58, 59, 60, 125
Niger-Congo, 4
Ntaryamira, Cyprien (President of Burundi), 22
Nyabingi, 15, 30, 117, 119, 120
Nyange, 36
Nyanza, 3, 74, 136
Nyaragongo, 1
Nyiginya clan, 135

Nyiginya Kingdom, 65, 72, 136
Nyina'rupfu, Mother Death, 33
Nyungwe National Park, 10
oral literature, 47, 48–49, 50–54, 58, 59,
    121, 141, 147; oral traditions, 15, 47,
    54, 55, 58, 59
ornaments, 63, 64, 69, 72, 74, 91

painting, 11, 63, 64, 65, 67, 72, 127
palace historians, 48, 55, 120, 140
PARMEHUTU (Parti du Mouvement de
    l'Emancipation Hutu), 17, 18
pastoralism, 125–26; pastoralists, 7, 9, 82,
    84, 126; pastoral songs, 135
patrilineal system, 14, 100, 107
Paul II, John (Pope), 42
PDI (Democratic Islamic Party), 41
Perraudin, André, Most Reverend, 36
poetry, 50, 124, 135, 145n3
poetry in Kinyarwanda, 51–52; royal
    poetry, 49, 51, 140
politics, 4, 11, 17, 34, 39, 41, 42, 43, 50,
    71, 111, 112, 138; political advisors, 7;
    political domination, 5, 28, 33; political
    institutions, 5, 50, 140; political
    leadership, 5, 18, 42, 129; political
    structure, 4, 6, 7; political system, 7,
    41, 47, 92, 128
polygyny. See marriage
Portuguese, 83
potters, 4, 6, 11, 71
pottery, 6, 8, 11, 63, 64, 65, 70–72, 77
Pottery Project. See CAURWA
proverbs, 47, 53–54, 59, 121, 133

Qur'anic schools, 39

RADER (Ressemblemt Démocratique
    Rwandais), 17, 18
radio, 22, 53, 55, 59, 61, 124, 125; Radio
    Rwanda, 55, 56; radio station, 55, 56, 58
rainmakers, 6, 28, 31
Ramadan, 40, 123
religion, 11, 14–16, 27–28, 36–43, 50, 55,
    63, 98, 131, 138; religious rituals, 7,
    32, 41, 42, 64, 131, 136
rice, 84, 88, 89, 94n6, 122
rock paintings, 64

Roman Catholic Church, 8, 16, 32, 37,
    38, 39, 42, 43, 57; Roman Catholic
    missionaries, 16, 32, 41, 128
Rouge, Khmer, 21
royal court, 31, 49, 65; royal dress, 91–92,
    93; royal regalia, 9
RTLM (Radio et Television Libres des
    Mille Collines), 56
ruharage, 138
Ruhengeri, 3, 6, 9, 74, 97
Rujugira, Cyirima, 9, 11
Rusumo Falls, 67
Rwabugiri, Kigeri, 11, 108
Rwanda, 15–20, 22–24, 27–43; Rwanda
    Nziza, 130, 147; Rwanda Rwacu, 130;
    Rwandan clans, 16, 32; Rwandan
    constitution, 20, 41; Rwandan culture,
    15, 29, 31, 34; Rwandan government,
    19; Rwandan independence, 18;
    Rwandans, 15, 23, 27–43, 48, 50–53;
    Rwandan society, 29, 32, 36, 38, 42,
    48, 49, 53; Rwandan unity, 37, 38
Ryangombe, 15, 30, 43n6, 117, 118, 119,
    120, 139
Ryangombe Rattle bells, 139

Sacred Fire, 118
sacred king, 5, 7
Samputu-Ingeli Dance Troupe, 145
Save, 33, 34
schools, 4, 9, 16, 18, 33, 41, 48, 52, 55,
    93, 124, 125, 127
sculpture, 63, 65, 66
secret societies, 103, 117, 119
shrines, 29, 30, 66
singers, 6, 140; professionals, 48, 49, 140;
    Twa singers, 136
soccer, 124, 125
social institutions, 97, 112, 119
socialization, 99–101, 115, 116, 124, 144
social status, 4, 10, 13, 15, 33, 41, 69, 91,
    93, 98
Society of Missionaries of Africa (White
    Fathers), 8
songs, 11, 13, 47, 85, 118, 119, 121,
    134–40; historical songs, 136; panegyric
    songs, 140; pastoral songs, 135; praise
    songs, 134–38; ritual songs, 142–43;

sacred songs, 135; songs about cows, 135; traditional songs, 134; Twa songs, 139

sorghum, 3, 13, 14, 29, 70, 82, 85, 86, 88, 118, 120, 121, 130

storytellers, 49, 55, 59, 121; storytelling, 8, 15, 49, 59, 100, 121, 123

Sunni, 39

Swahili, 7, 12, 34, 38, 39, 56, 65, 66, 83

taboos, 108–9, 112, 131

tambourinaires, 50, 92

Tanzania, 1, 19, 22, 39, 88

Taylor, Christopher, 88

tea, 11, 12

technology, 6, 11, 50, 77–78, 84, 129; iron technology, 6, 70; pottery technology, 72

Temps Nouveaux Urunana, 35

tobacco, 3, 12, 73

totems, *touchi*, 143

Tutsi, 319, 28–34, 64–74; Tutsi as cattle owners, 4, 5, 127; Tutsi and Christianity, 33–38, 41–42; Tutsi diet, 84–85; Tutsi as dynastic founders, 6; Tutsi and genocide, 20–24; Tutsi as *intore* dancers, 139; Tutsi and Islam, 38–40; Tutsi kings, 7, 9, 49, 50; Tutsi music, 33–38; Tutsi and *ubuhake*, 110; Tutsi warrior tradition, 50, 52, 135

Twa (Pygmy), 4, 5–6, 10, 11, 20, 22, 82, 85, 103, 109, 110, 112, 127, 134, 138, 139, 143, 144; Twa and clothing, 14, 65; Twa and genocide, 6; Twa as musicians, 134; Twa as potters, 6, 11, 71; Twa as singers, 136

ubudehe, 13, 85, 94n10, 121

ubuhake, 10, 110

Ubwiru, 7, 49

Uganda, 1, 2, 3, 5, 19, 22, 32, 39, 66, 82, 83, 88, 111, 123, 124

umuduri, 137, 138, 139

umuganura, 94n, 120, 142

UNAR (Union Nationale Rwandaise), 17, 18

urbanization, 75–77, 78, 97

Urewe pottery, 11

urwumana, 143

Uwilinguyimana, Agatha (Rwanda prime minister), 22

Vansina, Jan, 28, 50, 54, 72, 136, 141

villagization, 77

Virunga Mountains/region, 1, 2, 5, 6, 87

volcanoes, 1, 2, 28, 147

WAMY (World Assembly of Muslim Youth), 40

Warren, Fred and Lee, 134

Warren, Rick, 43

WCC (World Council of Churches), 38

Western education, 5, 8, 33, 34, 35, 48, 54, 59, 97, 111, 128, 129, 131

White Fathers, 8, 16, 32, 35

witchcraft, 31; witches, 31

women, 4, 8, 9, 31, 39, 65–72, 77, 83, 85, 89–91, 98, 101, 104–11, 119–20, 127; and change, 129–30; and dancing, 136, 141, 142; and modernity, 111–12; Women without Borders, 125

wood carving, 11, 63, 64, 65, 67–68, 72, 127

worldview, 27–29, 42

written literature, 48, 49, 50–54, 59

Yuhi III, 136

Yuhi IV, Gahindiro, 18

Yuhi V, Musinga, 33, 139

Zaza, 33, 34

Ziherambere, Dr. Eleazar, 64, 68

About the Author

JULIUS O. ADEKUNLE is Associate Professor of History and Anthropology at Monmouth University where he teaches various courses on Africa.